"CONGRESS SHALL MAKE NO LAW...ABRIDGING THE FREEDOM OF SPEECH, OR OF THE PRESS."

First Amendment to the U.S. Constitution

The basic foundation of our democracy is the First Amendment guarantee of freedom of expression. The Opposing Viewpoints Series is dedicated to the concept of this basic freedom and the idea that it is more important to practice it than to enshrine it.

CONTENTS

THE INFORMATION
REVOLUTION

OPPOSING VIEWPOINTS®

OTHER BOOKS OF RELATED INTEREST

THE INFORMATION
REVOLUTION
OPPOSING VIEWPOINTS®

David L. Bender, Publisher

Bruno Leone, Executive Editor

Brenda Stalcup, Managing Editor

Scott Barbour, Senior Editor

Paul A. Winters, Book Editor

Mary E. Williams, Assistant Editor

OPPOSING
VIEWPOINTS®
SERIES

Greenhaven Press, Inc., San Diego, California

Cover photo: Photodisc

Library of Congress Cataloging-in-Publication Data

Information revolution : opposing viewpoints / Paul A. Winters, book
    editor, Mary E. Williams, assistant editor.
        p.   cm. — (Opposing viewpoints series)
    Includes bibliographical references and index.
    ISBN 1-56510-801-9 (lib. : alk. paper). —
ISBN 1-56510-800-0 (pbk. : alk. paper)
    1. Information technology—Social aspects. 2. Information
society. I. Winters, Paul A., 1965–   . II. Williams, Mary E., 1960–   .
III. Series: Opposing viewpoints series (Unnumbered)
T58.5.I526 1998
303.48'33—dc21   98-5038
                                                                              CIP

Copyright ©1998 by Greenhaven Press, Inc.
Printed in the U.S.A.

Greenhaven Press, Inc., P.O. Box 289009
San Diego, CA 92198-9009

Why Consider Opposing Viewpoints?

"The only way in which a human being can make some approach to knowing the whole of a subject is by hearing what can be said about it by persons of every variety of opinion and studying all modes in which it can be looked at by every character of mind. No wise man ever acquired his wisdom in any mode but this."

John Stuart Mill

In our media-intensive culture it is not difficult to find differing opinions. Thousands of newspapers and magazines and dozens of radio and television talk shows resound with differing points of view. The difficulty lies in deciding which opinion to agree with and which "experts" seem the most credible. The more inundated we become with differing opinions and claims, the more essential it is to hone critical reading and thinking skills to evaluate these ideas. Opposing Viewpoints books address this problem directly by presenting stimulating debates that can be used to enhance and teach these skills. The varied opinions contained in each book examine many different aspects of a single issue. While examining these conveniently edited opposing views, readers can develop critical thinking skills such as the ability to compare and contrast authors' credibility, facts, argumentation styles, use of persuasive techniques, and other stylistic tools. In short, the Opposing Viewpoints Series is an ideal way to attain the higher-level thinking and reading skills so essential in a culture of diverse and contradictory opinions.

In addition to providing a tool for critical thinking, Opposing Viewpoints books challenge readers to question their own strongly held opinions and assumptions. Most people form their opinions on the basis of upbringing, peer pressure, and personal, cultural, or professional bias. By reading carefully balanced opposing views, readers must directly confront new ideas as well as the opinions of those with whom they disagree. This is not to simplistically argue that everyone who reads opposing views will—or should—change his or her opinion. Instead, the series enhances readers' understanding of their own views by encouraging confrontation with opposing ideas. Careful examination of others' views can lead to the readers' understanding of the logical inconsistencies in their own opinions, perspective on why they hold an opinion, and the consideration of the possibility that their opinion requires further evaluation.

EVALUATING OTHER OPINIONS

To ensure that this type of examination occurs, Opposing Viewpoints books present all types of opinions. Prominent spokespeople on different sides of each issue as well as well-known professionals from many disciplines challenge the reader. An additional goal of the series is to provide a forum for other, less known, or even unpopular viewpoints. The opinion of an ordinary person who has had to make the decision to cut off life support from a terminally ill relative, for example, may be just as valuable and provide just as much insight as a medical ethicist's professional opinion. The editors have two additional purposes in including these less known views. One, the editors encourage readers to respect others' opinions—even when not enhanced by professional credibility. It is only by reading or listening to and objectively evaluating others' ideas that one can determine whether they are worthy of consideration. Two, the inclusion of such viewpoints encourages the important critical thinking skill of objectively evaluating an author's credentials and bias. This evaluation will illuminate an author's reasons for taking a particular stance on an issue and will aid in readers' evaluation of the author's ideas.

As series editors of the Opposing Viewpoints Series, it is our hope that these books will give readers a deeper understanding of the issues debated and an appreciation of the complexity of even seemingly simple issues when good and honest people disagree. This awareness is particularly important in a democratic society such as ours in which people enter into public debate to determine the common good. Those with whom one disagrees should not be regarded as enemies but rather as people whose views deserve careful examination and may shed light on one's own.

Thomas Jefferson once said that "difference of opinion leads to inquiry, and inquiry to truth." Jefferson, a broadly educated man, argued that "if a nation expects to be ignorant and free . . . it expects what never was and never will be." As individuals and as a nation, it is imperative that we consider the opinions of others and examine them with skill and discernment. The Opposing Viewpoints Series is intended to help readers achieve this goal.

David L. Bender & Bruno Leone,
Series Editors

Greenhaven Press anthologies primarily consist of previously published material taken from a variety of sources, including periodicals, books, scholarly journals, newspapers, government documents, and position papers from private and public organizations. These original sources are often edited for length and to ensure their accessibility for a young adult audience. The anthology editors also change the original titles of these works in order to clearly present the main thesis of each viewpoint and to explicitly indicate the opinion presented in the viewpoint. These alterations are made in consideration of both the reading and comprehension levels of a young adult audience. Every effort is made to ensure that Greenhaven Press accurately reflects the original intent of the authors included in this anthology.

INTRODUCTION

"The United States stands today in the midst of one of the great revolutions in recorded history: the Information Age."

—U.S. Advisory Council on the National Information Infrastructure

In 1438, the German inventor Johann Gutenberg wanted to find a cheaper, quicker way to produce the Bible, which had previously been hand copied. He created the type mold, which made printing from movable type practical for the first time—and thereby ushered in a new era of increased literacy and advances in scientific knowledge. Centuries of scientific advances, in turn, eventually led to innovations in machine design that helped to launch the Industrial Revolution of the nineteenth and twentieth centuries—a period of dramatic economic and technological change bolstered by the speed and efficiency of mechanization.

By the 1940s, breakthroughs in the development of calculating machines and electronic circuitry culminated in the invention of the first modern digital computers, which were originally designed for military purposes during World War II. These room-size computers performed a few thousand calculations per second and took hours to complete complex mathematical problems. By the mid-1990s, however, lightweight, portable computers that could perform millions of calculations per second had been developed and people used them for personal finance, business, and education. Satellite and wireless technologies could deliver up-to-date information from around the world into homes, businesses, and other public and private institutions. Common electronic appliances and services such as televisions, telephones, radios, and computer networks gave much of the population unprecedented high-speed communications capabilities. Many experts proclaim that these still-evolving electronic, satellite, and information technologies are generating changes in human history as profound as the effects wrought by the Industrial Revolution. According to the U.S. Advisory Council on the National Information Infrastructure, the information revolution is "changing fundamentally the ways in which people work, learn, communicate, care for their own health, and create their home lives."

The world's fastest growing communications conduit, the Internet, is the current cutting edge of the information revolution. The Internet is an international consolidation of several thousand computer networks serving more than 50 million users. Its most popular system, the World Wide Web, is a compilation of business, government, educational, and personal "sites" that feature electronic "pages" of text and images. Internet users can access multiple sources of information with software "browsers" and "search engines" that navigate through the Web; they can also contact other Internet users with electronic mail (e-mail) and interact with people who share their interests through on-line discussion groups, bulletin boards, and "chat rooms."

The Internet offers greatly enhanced educational, commercial, and personal opportunities. Through the World Wide Web, Internet users can draw on the educational resources of various libraries, think tanks, businesses, government offices, research institutions, and advocacy organizations. On-line interactive networks enable students and workers to have discussions with globally dispersed experts and educators. Members of "virtual" communities—Internet users united by a common interest or commitment—can interact over time zones and vast geographical distances. In the words of Joel L. Swerdlow, a senior writer for *National Geographic*,

> The Internet pushes life beyond the old barriers of time and space. Here you can roam around the world without leaving home. Make new friends. Communicate with astronauts as they circle the earth. Exchange the results of laboratory experiments with a colleague overseas. Read stock quotes. Buy clothes. Research a term paper. Stay out of the office, conducting business via a computer that becomes your virtual office.

Some Internet enthusiasts contend, furthermore, that the ultimate benefit of this enhanced access to data and long-distance communication will be a flowering of knowledge informed by the values of diverse communities and cultures.

Whether knowledge is gained through the Internet's fast track to information is debated, however. Criticisms of the Internet often center on the increasing amount of unedited data available on the World Wide Web. As Clifford Stoll, author of *Silicon Snake Oil: Second Thoughts on the Information Highway*, contends, "Lacking editors, reviewers, or critics, the Internet has become a wasteland of unfiltered data. You don't know what to ignore and what's worth reading." Some critics argue that the seemingly unlimited amount of information and ideas on the Web creates more confusion than clarity, particularly when younger or unsophisticated Internet users neglect to question the credibility of website sources. Stoll and others maintain, furthermore, that the Internet's so-called virtual communities are a poor substitute for actual communities. These critics contend that the proliferation of

Internet discussion groups and bulletin boards encourages people to seclude themselves in front of a computer screen. "Discount the fawning technoburble about virtual communities," Stoll asserts. "Computers and networks isolate us from one another." Instead of creating alternative communities, he argues, the avoidance of human contact caused by Internet use could actually widen existing societal and cultural divisions.

The Internet is a new and evolving technology, so its ultimate effect on the acquisition of knowledge and on communities remains to be seen. As more and more people gain increased access to information through the Internet and other developing communications technologies, however, the social impact of the information revolution will continue to foster debate. *The Information Revolution: Opposing Viewpoints* spotlights this ongoing controversy in the following chapters: Will the Information Revolution Benefit Society? Will the Information Revolution Transform Education? Will the Information Revolution Transform Work? Are Rights Threatened in the Information Age? Exploring these questions will provoke readers to assess the possible consequences of new and evolving information technologies.

CHAPTER 1

WILL THE INFORMATION REVOLUTION BENEFIT SOCIETY?

CHAPTER PREFACE

At a speech delivered to the International Telecommunications Union in Buenos Aires, Argentina, in March 1994, U.S. vice president Al Gore first unveiled the idea of a Global Information Infrastructure (GII). He describes the potential GII as an international communications network consisting of several technological innovations, including computers, databases, telephones, televisions, satellites, and fiber optics. The goal of such an infrastructure, Gore proposes, would be "to transmit information with the speed of light from the largest city to the smallest village on every continent in every part of our world." Because of its ability to transcend "the barriers of time and distance, of wealth and poverty, of developed and developing countries," Gore claims that the GII would forever change the nature of global interactions and foster economic development, educational opportunities, scientific breakthroughs, and cross-cultural communication. Supporters of the GII envision it as an information superhighway that could, for instance, allow all students access to the world's prestigious libraries, enable entrepreneurs to buy and sell goods in a virtual global marketplace, relay information to medical personnel treating the sick in underdeveloped nations, and promote worldwide democracy.

Skeptics, however, question the feasibility of a Global Information Infrastructure. For example, they point out that two-thirds of the world's population have no access to telephone service, and three-fourths of the global populace live in nations with ten or fewer telephones for every one hundred people. While efforts are being made to improve international access to telecommunications, the World Bank estimates that a total of $250 billion would be needed to build or modernize telecommunications networks in developing countries. Procuring the capital to build these networks has been difficult because investors are discouraged by the lack of skilled management in third world countries. While Western and industrialized nations will be connected to a vast information infrastructure, financial and social obstacles will probably prevent most of the world's people from acquiring advanced telecommunications access, critics of the proposed GII maintain.

Experts and analysts continue to disagree about the potential benefits of the information revolution. The authors of the following chapter present additional debates on this timely issue.

| "The phenomenal, instantaneous global access both to other people and, in the end, to the totality of mankind's knowledge, will have a profound impact on humanity."

THE INFORMATION REVOLUTION CAN BENEFIT SOCIETY

Michael Spindler

Computer and network communication technology will transform society, Michael Spindler predicts in the following viewpoint. Society will benefit from this technological revolution, he argues, if individuals use information technology to learn and to connect to others rather than simply to entertain themselves. Spindler is the former president and CEO of Apple Computer Corporation.

As you read, consider the following questions:

1. According to Spindler, what are the three main trends of technology in the information age?
2. Why will there be an increasing variety of information appliances for businesses and homes, according to Spindler?
3. In the author's opinion, how can information be both a blessing and a curse?

Reprinted from "Taking the Message Back from the Medium," by Michael Spindler, *New Perspectives Quarterly*, Spring 1995, by permission of Blackwell Publishers, Inc.

Technology has always been the root cause of economic and social change. This time around it is no different. When Johann Gutenberg invented the moveable type in Europe, the pessimists said it was bad because all the scribes would lose their jobs. The optimists said it was great because it would enable the distribution of books in libraries. The politicians said we can't have anything unless we create a law. And who was right? Well, the scribes did lose their jobs, but they were the ones who started the European wine industry. So, you cannot stop technology from moving forward.

The main trends shaping the shifting technology landscape in this new information age are profound:

- The complete shift from analog to digital technology in everything from telephone-switching systems to transmission to content creation and packaging and the end-user information devices;
- The impact of miniaturization technology on the size of products and the pervasiveness of mobile products;
- The continuous change and pace of technological deployment.

EARLY VISIONS OF A COMPUTER INFORMATION NETWORK

The new information appliances will be varied—smart communicators, multimedia personal computers (PCs), recepto-boxes, game consoles, TV sets and smart-phones. Already in the 1960s, foresightful people realized that the destiny of the computer was to be an interactive, complementary amplifier of human thought rather than remaining a mere transaction machine. They understood that if we could only pervasively network human beings and information appliances through computers we would create the universal information utility to which most human commerce, both intellectual and commercial, would flow.

Today, it is clear that the access to networking is not a problem at all—the Internet experience has shown that.

Information appliances for business organizations as well as residential use will continue to fragment because of different consumer constraints, such as the amount of discretionary income, and preferences for viewing and accessing multimedia information. This is particularly so for residential use because of varying life-style choices such as working at home. All this will lead to a fragmentation of application, rather than one "killer" application that applies to all circumstances.

How many information appliances will we have at home and which one will be in highest use? Will it still be the television set? The television set has not acquired much intelligence in the past 10 years. It has remained a passive receiver for broadcast media. The basic multimedia architecture and versatility of a personal computer may provide a much better platform for a variety of end-use appliances.

A Civilization's Highest Calling

Cyberspace is the land of knowledge, and the exploration of that land can be a civilization's truest, highest calling. The opportunity is now before us to empower every person to pursue that calling in his or her own way.

The challenge is as daunting as the opportunity is great. The Third Wave [the information age] has profound implications for the nature and meaning of property, of the marketplace, of community and of individual freedom. As it emerges, it shapes new codes of behavior that move each organism and institution—family, neighborhood, church group, company, government, nation—inexorably beyond standardization and centralization, as well as beyond the materialist's obsession with energy, money and control.

Turning the economics of mass-production inside out, new information technologies are driving the financial costs of diversity—both product and personal—down toward zero, "demassifying" our institutions and our culture. Accelerating demassification creates the potential for vastly increased human freedom.

Esther Dyson, George Gilder, Jay Keyworth, and Alvin Toffler, *New Perspectives Quarterly*, Fall 1994.

The phenomenal, instantaneous global access both to other people and, in the end, to the totality of mankind's knowledge, will have a profound impact on humanity. More and more people will possess personal information access. People will have universal e-mail phones and fax numbers that will stay with them for life and be usable no matter where in the world they are.

Massive cultural shifts will occur as they did around paper based information publishing, the invention of the telephone or television. We will shift from a pure broadcast-mat culture to a much more interactive society, developing ever more diverse communities of interests where people who otherwise had no contact can interact.

How to Cope with the Information Revolution

We do not yet understand the real impact of the global information society. The critical element for individuals moving into the future is not to obtain a Ph.D. in information science, but to acquire a point of view of how information can best be useful to them.

Information, or more accurately, being informed, can be both a blessing and a curse. We crave more information; at the same time we feel inundated, intruded upon and lacking control.

The key concern as we move forward is to ensure that the real end-user remain in control of the outcome. The consumer, not some techno-buffs, must remain the sole judge of demand and consumption in this media-rich world coming into being.

I sincerely and personally hope that all of this doesn't mean we are moving into an information environment which more and more resembles the game "Trivial Pursuit." We need to have a culture that sustains the emotions, friendships and interpersonal connections necessary so that this technology does not become intimidating. As has been demonstrated many times over, a culture can survive misinformation and false information. It has not yet been proven, however, whether a culture can survive by taking the measure of the world in 30-second sound-bites.

My hope is that we do not end up with a societal model where five percent of the nation's population is well-educated, well-informed and earning good wages while the rest simply amuse themselves to death.

> "Perhaps the positives of infotech will
> outweigh the negatives, but I
> wouldn't bet on it."

THE INFORMATION REVOLUTION MAY NOT BENEFIT SOCIETY

Michael Marien

In the following viewpoint, Michael Marien lists ten ways that the information revolution will negatively impact society. The most serious problem, he argues, is that a glut of trivia and entertainment may crowd out useful and beneficial information. Marien is the editor of *Future Survey*, a monthly publication of the World Future Society.

As you read, consider the following questions:
1. In Marien's opinion, how is the information revolution harmful to privacy?
2. Why does the author believe that the information revolution is bad for democracy?
3. According to the author, how does the problem of infoglut affect society?

Reprinted from "Top Ten Reasons the Information Revolution Is Bad for Us," by Michael Marien, Futurist, January/February 1997, by permission of the World Future Society, 7910 Woodmont Ave., Suite 450, Bethesda, MD 20814; (301) 656-8274; fax: (301) 951-0394; http://www.wfs.org/wfs.

There is no doubt at all that an information revolution is happening, both for better and for worse. But there is considerable doubt about whether the positive impacts outweigh the negative impacts, both now and in the future.

Here is my top-10 list of negatives; I'll start at the bottom and work up to the number-one problem.

10. The information revolution is bad for equality, creating ever-greater social gaps within and between nations.

9. It's bad for quality of life. It speeds the pace of life and makes time increasingly scarce.

8. It's bad for privacy. Interlinked databases have your name, your numbers, and much more about you. But privacy is a cultural construct, and maybe we'll learn to live with this new invasion, even with cameras on every lamppost.

7. It's bad for democracy—so far, at least. Of course, there's the promise of enhanced citizen participation and electronic town meetings, but don't confuse the potential with the reality. In a recent poll, only 33% of adults could name their congressman, let alone what he or she stands for. Ironically, as a society becomes more complex, people are turned off of politics and turned on to an expanding variety of electronic entertainment.

THE INFORMATION REVOLUTION IMPACTS THE ENVIRONMENT

6. It's bad for the environment. The sustainable society, which is something we need in the future, is being displaced by the glitzy Information Society, which is something we don't really need, and perhaps don't really want. The Information Society is a distraction from the necessity of building a sustainable society.

5. It's bad for jobs. We haven't seen much impact yet, because our society is still wedded to phony unemployment statistics that understate those who have part-time work and want full-time work, and ignores those who are prematurely retired and those who have dropped out of the labor force. But as the new software becomes more widespread, we can expect more unemployment and under-employment.

4. It's bad for national security. We have the capacity to wage infowar, but we are also equally vulnerable to infowar and infoterrorism.

3. It is bad for law and order. Computer crime is a major cost for business and government, and much of it is not recorded. Could losses from cybercrime be one of the reasons that recent productivity gains are small and our economy is only performing so-so?

2. It is bad for the future. There seems to be a decline in the

quantity and quality of serious futures thinking. Why? Quite possibly because infotech and infosociety have made the future unappealing and created a reaction against the future by those who, unconsciously or not, want to stop the world and get off.

INFORMATION OVERLOAD

1. The number-one negative is that having much more information is bad for our heads. It is bad because it produces infoglut, which may well be the greatest under-studied problem of our time.

Infoglut is not a static matter. It's been estimated in the *Encyclopedia of the Future* that scientific information doubles about every 12 years and general information doubles about every two and a half years. But the really good stuff, the most important knowledge that should steer society, communities, enterprises, and individual lives, is increasingly in short supply relative to other information devoted to entertainment and commercial interests.

INFORMATION DEPENDENCY

Divorced from the cognitive structure that is knowledge and the reflectively internalized knowledge that is wisdom, information makes us dumb. It is a distraction—from the Latin verb *distrahere*, which means to draw away, disperse, or squander our capacity for thought. Today the poor of the urban underclass are said to suffer from radical dependency. The person who begins and ends the day with television, all-talk-all-the-time radio, or hitting Web sites is cognitively crippled by a comparable dependency. Such people are burdened by an overload of opinions, but they have no opinions, meaning reflective judgments, that are truly their own. They cannot know what they think since they have not heard the latest thought and, by definition, never will.

Richard John Neuhaus, *Forbes ASAP*, December 2, 1996.

The impacts of infoglut include the devaluing of information as overload leads to boredom. It leads to stress and more work to keep up, with the loss of sleep as a consequence, leading in turn to lost productivity in the workplace and the classroom.

Suffice it to say that we are hurtling into a new era with very little serious analysis or opposition. Perhaps the positives of infotech will outweigh the negatives, but I wouldn't bet on it. Even if the positives outweighed the negatives, it is wise to take the pessimistic, skeptical position, because there is so much at stake.

"Information overload has emerged as
a genuine threat."

SOCIETY IS SUFFERING FROM INFORMATION OVERLOAD

David Shenk

With innovations in computer and communication technology
in the late twentieth century, argues David Shenk in the following viewpoint, individuals have quickly become deluged with
more information than they can process. Because much of this
data is unwanted, useless, and trivial, he contends, it distracts
people and prevents them from accumulating useful information, thereby producing increasing feelings of stress. Shenk is
the author of *Data Smog: Surviving the Information Glut*, from which
this viewpoint is excerpted.

As you read, consider the following questions:
1. How does Shenk define spamming?
2. In the author's opinion, what is the great paradox of the
   information revolution?
3. How does "data smog" affect individuals, according to the
   author?

When the definitive history of the information revolution is written years from now, one of the milestones will be urban sociologist Richard Meier's warning, in 1962, that society would face a deluge of data within fifty years. Another will be the April 1994 spamming by Canter & Siegel. In Internet jargon, *spamming* is the wanton mass-transmittal of unsolicited electronic messages. (The term is derived from a comedy skit by the absurdist troupe Monty Python in which unsuspecting diners are informed that the restaurant menu includes "egg and bacon, egg sausage and bacon, egg and Spam, egg bacon and Spam, egg bacon sausage and Spam, Spam bacon sausage and Spam, Spam egg Spam Spam bacon and Spam [and so on].") When, in the early 1990s, it was noticed that certain individuals got a kick out of interrupting text-based Net dialogues with useless and irrelevant drivel, the term "spam" seemed apt.

THE BIRTH OF SPAMMING

On April 12, 1994, Laurence Canter and Martha Siegel, a married team of Arizona lawyers, took spamming to an entirely new level of abuse when they posted to over 6,000 Usenet newsgroups an unsolicited commercial offer to help immigrants enter an upcoming "Green Card lottery." (Usenet is a portion of the Internet that provides discussion forums on thousands of specific topics—Japanese animation, the music of Bob Dylan, college basketball, environmental politics, and so on. Archery aficionados from all over the world can stay in touch with one another without regard to geography. Newsgroups are forums for super-specialized dialogue, and off-topic contributions are thoroughly unwelcome.) The international outrage over Canter & Siegel's intrusion—regarded as doubly obnoxious because it was not done in the interests of sharing information but merely to make money—was immediate and overwhelming. So many angry protests were electronically dispatched to Canter & Siegel's Internet service provider that its host computers crashed more than fifteen times. Though the system administrator quickly canceled Canter & Siegel's account, the proud pioneers of major league spamming went on to spam some more, boast about spamming on television, and even write a book (published by HarperCollins) called *How to Make a Fortune on the Information Superhighway.*

With unsolicited commercial messages—junk e-mail—now showing up in people's boxes every day, it appears that spamming is here to stay. And so, clearly, is the acute sensation (the grating irritation) of being overloaded with unwanted information. The reaction to Canter & Siegel demonstrates that today, many people know—and feel—what Richard Meier warned about thirty-five years ago. Information overload has emerged as a genuine threat.

One certainly does not have to be online to experience it, however. At home, at work, and even at play, communication has engulfed our lives. To be human is to traffic in enormous chunks of data. "Tens of thousands of words daily pulse through our beleaguered brains," says philosopher Philip Novak, "accompanied by a massive amount of other auditory and visual stimuli. In every moment of the audio-visual orgy of our highly informed days, the brain handles a massive amount of electrical traffic. No wonder we feel burnt."

THE PROLIFERATION OF INFORMATION

While information overload has surely been accelerated and highlighted by the popularization of the Internet, it is by no means limited to computers or to life in the 1990s. In his 1979 lyrical, fabulist novel, *If on a winter's night a traveler*, Italo Calvino mischievously relates the sensation of being confronted with more information than one knows how to handle:

> In the shop window, you have promptly identified the cover with the title you were looking for. Following this visual trail, you have forced your way through the shop past the thick barricade of Books You Haven't Read, which were frowning at you from the tables and shelves, trying to cow you. But you know you must never allow yourself to be awed . . . but then you are attacked by the infantry of Books That If You Had More Than One Life You Would Certainly Also Read But Unfortunately Your Days Are Numbered . . . you come up beneath the towers of the fortress, where other troops are holding out:
>
> the Books You've Been Planning To Read For Ages,
>
> the Books You've Been Hunting For Years Without Success,
>
> the Books Dealing With Something You're Working On At The Moment,
>
> the Books You Want To Own So They'll Be Handy Just In Case,
>
> the Books You Could Put Aside To Maybe Read This Summer . . .

This is the flip side of what we commonly refer to as our "wealth of information." Information used to be as rare and precious as gold. (It is estimated that one weekday edition of today's *New York Times* contains more information than the average person in seventeenth-century England was likely to come across in an entire lifetime.) Now it is so inexpensive and plentiful that most of it ends up being remaindered and shredded, as if it is worthless garbage.

Therein lies the first great paradox of information glut—we are becoming so information-rich that we take much of what we have for granted. When information wasn't so easily acquired, explains theater director Peter Sellars, "the actual act of finding something had value." But "where there is no pilgrimage, the information itself is debased, devalued and dehumanized. . . . We have everything at our fingertips but we don't value anything."

THE FIRST LAW OF DATA SMOG

Information, once rare and cherished like caviar, is now plentiful and taken for granted like potatoes.

Still, the concept of too much information seems odd and vaguely inhuman. This is because, in evolutionary-historical terms, this weed in our information landscape has just sprouted—it is only about fifty years old.

Up until then, more information was almost always a good thing. For nearly 100,000 years leading up to this century, information technology has been an unambiguous virtue as a means of sustaining and developing culture. Information and communications have made us steadily healthier, wealthier, more tolerant. Because of information, we understand more about how to overcome the basic challenges of life. Food is more abundant. Our physical structures are sturdier, more reliable. Our societies are more stable, as we have learned how to make political systems function. Our citizens are freer, thanks to a wide dissemination of information that has empowered the individual. Dangerous superstitions and false notions have been washed away: Communicating quickly with people helps to overcome our fear of them and diminishes the likelihood of conflict.

But around the time of the first atomic bomb, something happened that did not halt but did contaminate this progress. Not only did humans begin to invent machines with a whole new level of power and complexity behind them. We also crossed an important rubicon: We began to produce information much faster than we could process it.

This had never happened before. For 100,000 years the three fundamental stages of the communications process—production, distribution, and processing—had been more or less in synch with one another. By and large, over our long history, people have been able to examine and consider information about as quickly as it could be created and circulated. This equipoise lasted through an astonishing range of communications media—the drum, smoke signal, cave painting, horse, town crier, carrier pigeon, newspaper, photograph, telegraph, telephone, radio, and film.

COMPUTERS AND THE OVERPRODUCTION OF INFORMATION

But in the mid–twentieth century this graceful synchrony was abruptly knocked off track with the introduction of computers, microwave transmissions, television, and satellites. These hyper-production and hyper-distribution mechanisms surged ahead of human processing ability, leaving us with a permanent processing deficit, what Finnish sociologist Jaako Lehtonen calls an "information discrepancy."

Jim Borgman. Reprinted by special permission of King Features Syndicate.

In this way, in a very short span of natural history, we have vaulted from a state of information scarcity to one of information surplus—from drought to flood in the geological blink of an eye. In 1850, 4 percent of American workers handled information for a living; now most do, and information processing (as opposed to material goods) now accounts for more than half of the U.S. gross national product. Data has become more plentiful, more speedy (computer processing speed has doubled every two years for the last thirty years), and more dense (from 1965 to 1995, the average network television advertisement shrunk from 53.1 seconds to 25.4 seconds and the average TV news "soundbite" shrunk from 42.3 seconds to 8.3 seconds; meanwhile, over the same period, the number of ads per network TV minute increased from 1.1 to 2.4).

Information has also become a lot cheaper—to produce, to manipulate, to disseminate. Consequently, virtually anyone can very easily become an information-glutton. We now face the prospect of information obesity.

Just as fat has replaced starvation as this nation's number one dietary concern, information overload has replaced information scarcity as an important new emotional, social, and political problem. "The real issue for future technology," says Columbia's Eli Noam, "does not appear to be production of information, and certainly not transmission. Almost anybody can *add* information. The difficult question is how to *reduce* it."

THE EASE OF CAPTURING INFORMATION

Action photographers often use a machine called a "motor drive" that attaches to 35mm cameras. The motor drive allows a photographer to shoot many separate exposures in any given second just by keeping his or her finger on a button. *Click-click-click-click-click....*

What an elegant metaphor for our age: With virtually no effort and for relatively little cost, we can capture as much information as we want. The capturing requires very little planning or forethought, and in fact is built right into the design of our machines. With a thumb and index finger, we effortlessly Copy and Paste sentences, paragraphs, books. After writing e-mail, we "carbon copy" it to one or one hundred others. The same goes for the photocopy machine, onto which we simply enter whatever number of copies we desire. *Would you like those collated and stapled? It's no bother.*

Only as an afterthought do we confront the consequences of such a low transaction cost. "E-mail is an open duct into your central nervous system," says Michael Dertouzos, director of the Massachusetts Institute of Technology's Laboratory for Computer Science, exaggerating playfully to make a serious point. "It occupies the brain and reduces productivity."

With information production not only increasing, but *accelerating*, there is no sign that processing will ever catch up. We have quite suddenly mutated into a radically different culture, a civilization that trades in and survives on stylized communication. We no longer hunt or gather; few of us farm or assemble. Instead, we negotiate, we network, we interface. And as we enjoy the many fruits of this burgeoning information civilization, we also have to learn to compensate for the new and permanent side effects of what sociologists, in an academic understatement, call a "message dense" society.

USEFUL INFORMATION VS. NOISE

Audio buffs have long been familiar with the phrase *signal-to-noise ratio*. It is engineering parlance for measuring the quality of a sound system by comparing the amount of desired audio signal to the amount of unwanted noise leaking through. In the information age, *signal-to-noise* has also become a useful way to think about social health and stability. How much of the information in our midst is useful, and how much of it gets in the way? What is our signal-to-noise ratio?

We know that the ratio has diminished of late, and that the character of information has changed: As we have accrued more and more of it, information has emerged not only as a currency, but also as a pollutant.

- In 1971 the average American was targeted by at least 560 daily advertising messages. Twenty years later, that number had risen sixfold, to 3,000 messages per day.
- In the office, an average of 60 percent of each person's time is now spent processing documents.
- Paper consumption per capita in the United States tripled from 1940 to 1980 (from 200 to 600 pounds), and tripled *again* from 1980 to 1990 (to 1,800 pounds).
- In the 1980s, third-class mail (used to send publications) grew thirteen times faster than population growth.
- The typical business manager is said to read 1 million words per week.
- As of 1990, more than 30,000 telemarketing companies employed 18 million Americans and generated $400 billion in annual sales.

Let us call this unexpected, unwelcome part of our atmosphere "data smog," an expression for the noxious muck and druck of the information age. Data smog gets in the way; it crowds out quiet moments, and obstructs much-needed contemplation. It spoils conversation, literature, and even entertainment. It thwarts skepticism, rendering us less sophisticated as consumers and citizens. It stresses us out.

DATA SMOG

Data smog is not just the pile of unsolicited catalogs and spam arriving daily in our home and electronic mailboxes. It is also information that we pay handsomely for, that we *crave*—the seductive, mesmerizing quick-cut television ads and the twenty-four-hour up-to-the-minute news flashes. It is the faxes we request as well as the ones we don't; it is the misdialed numbers and drippy sales calls we get during dinnertime; but it is also the Web sites we eagerly visit before and after dinner, the pile of magazines we pore through every month, and the dozens of channels we flip through whenever we get a free moment.

The blank spaces and silent moments in life are fast disappearing. Mostly because we have asked for it, media is everywhere. Televisions, telephones, radios, message beepers, and an assortment of other modern communication and navigational aids are now as ubiquitous as roads and tennis shoes—anywhere humans can go, all forms of media now follow: onto trains, planes, automobiles, into hotel bathrooms, along jogging paths and mountain trails, on bikes and boats. . . .

Information and entertainment now conform to our every orientation: Giant television screens adorn stadiums and surround theatrical stages; more ordinary-size TVs hang from ceilings in bars and airport lounges; mini-TVs are installed in front of individual seats in new airliners. Cellular telephone conversation creates a new ambiance for sidewalks and hallways. Beepers and laptop computers follow us home and come with us on vacation.

Meanwhile, the flavor of the information has also changed. It's no longer a matter of mono *versus* stereo or black and white *versus* color. TV and computer screens have been transformed into a hypnotic visual sizzle that MTV aptly calls "eye candy." With hypermedia, "dense TV," and split-screens providing a multiplicity of images at once, straining our attention has become one of our most popular forms of entertainment.

We've heard a lot lately about the moral decay evident in our entertainment packaging. But it isn't so much the content of the messages that should worry us as much as their ubiquity, and it is critical to realize that information doesn't have to be unwanted and unattractive to be harmful.

"Contrary to popular impressions of late twentieth-century society, . . . our mentalities are dealing quite well with the big, booming, buzzing world."

SOCIETY IS NOT SUFFERING FROM INFORMATION OVERLOAD

Paul Levinson

Arguments that technology threatens society ignore the fact that humans have long used technology to defend themselves against natural threats, Paul Levinson maintains in the following viewpoint. If society is facing an overload of information produced by computers, he contends, it is not because humans are incapable of processing the volumes of information but because most people have not yet developed technological systems for categorizing and managing the flow of information. Levinson is the president of Connected Education, a group in White Plains, New York, that promotes the use of computers in education. He is also the author of *Learning Cyberspace: Essays on the Evolution of Media and the New Education* and the 1997 book *The Soft Edge: A Natural History and Future of the Information Revolution*.

As you read, consider the following questions:

1. In Levinson's opinion, what are the biggest threats to humanity?
2. According to the author, what is the decisive factor in whether technology is used for good or evil?
3. How does the mind work to digest information, according to Levinson?

From "On Behalf of Humanity," by Paul Levinson. This article appeared in the March 1996 issue, and is reprinted with permission from, the *World & I*, a publication of The Washington Times Corporation, copyright ©1996.

A rational examination of technology needs to begin with a recognition of its role in the living world. We find that long before humans arose on this planet, its life forms manipulated their environments in all manner of ways that we still see much in evidence today, in beaver dams and spider webs and bird nests. Indeed, technology is a fundamental strategy of life itself, not only responding to external environments but reshaping them on behalf of the organisms it serves.

Not surprisingly, the infusion of human mentality into the ancient biological process of technology—its animation with our penchants for dream and design—has lifted it into something that has literally transformed our entire planet perhaps more than all living processes before it. And with this human impulse writ large, and its capacity for destruction as well as construction, aggression as well as affection, has come all kinds of amplified perils. A gun is more dangerous than a fist or a claw, and an atomic bomb trumps them all in threat to ourselves and our planet.

REASONABLE AND UNREASONABLE CONCERNS ABOUT TECHNOLOGY

Reasonable people thus find themselves not only appreciative of technology's benefits, but concerned about its dangers—concerned, to be more specific, about potentials for the human misuse of technology. But as often happens in matters so fundamental to human existence, what begins as a reasonable concern can quickly escalate into critiques and denunciations that lose sight of the underlying realities. This has happened in the view of Jacques Ellul (The Technological Society, 1954) and others who claim that technology is essentially autonomous and out of human control; that it is in intrinsic and profound opposition to the natural world; that it is thus the leading source of danger to human beings and planet earth.

Such views not only miss the natural evolutionary situation of technology indicated above. They overlook the fact that by far the worse threats to humanity are and always have been non-technological in origin: disease, drought, earthquake, and all manner of natural calamities that befall us. And they overlook the only effective response we can mount to these dangers—the essential role of technology in the dissemination and organization of information, in the growth of knowledge, medicine, agriculture, and the myriad activities we perform daily.

Common sense, as the British philosopher G.E. Moore aptly counseled at the turn of the nineteenth century, is a good place to begin any serious investigation. The common sense view of technology on the question of its good and evil consequences is that it is most like a knife—which can easily be used for good, as in cutting food, or bad, as in cutting people. The knife, and technology in general, are thus in this view thought to be thoroughly under human control.

Let's explore this a little further. Can we think of technologies that are intrinsically biased—to use the phrase introduced by Harold Innis (*The Bias of Communication*, 1951)—toward good or bad purposes? Well, surely a gun seems weighted toward doing people harm; and a pillow seems intended as an innocuously beneficial convenience.

But notwithstanding their biases toward bad and good, a gun or a pillow can also be used for an opposite purpose: A gun serves a good end when used by a hunter to procure food; and a pillow can be no less an instrument of murder when the cause of death is deliberate suffocation.

So it seems that guns and pillows are but special kinds of knives: They may be intrinsically weighted toward evil and good, respectively, but ultimately they can be made to perform (or not perform) in whatever ways humans intend.

Good vs. Bad Technology?

Let's up the stakes a little more. Are any technologies so unremittingly bad, or good, that they defy any and all human intention in the opposite direction? In other words, do any technologies qualify as "superguns" or "superpillows"?

Nuclear weapons are the obvious supergun. They certainly cannot work as a direct provider of food; they perhaps can defend a just society from attack by an unjust, but when actually used they entail a horrendous cost to both innocent people and the earth as a whole. Nonetheless, nuclear energy, of which nuclear weapons are a subset, has uses in medicine and perhaps in providing energy via fusion (safer than fission) reactors. Furthermore, as physicist Freeman Dyson once suggested, nuclear weapons themselves could be hauled off the earth—once we develop our shuttle-craft technology enough—and assembled in orbit to power the first starship to Alpha Centauri. This strategy would at once remove these weapons from our planet and advance our exploration of the cosmos. Certainly in light of these real medical and hypothetical space-exploration uses, nuclear weapons and their associated technologies are significantly less than 100 percent, unremittingly inapplicable to good purposes.

What about the other side of the street: Can we specify a technology that is 100 percent, unswervingly good in its consequences? Vaccines would seem a clear example of that: Even technology's severest critics are prone to see nothing amiss in the eradication of smallpox. But, alas, we also know that disease-fighting technology can easily be turned into disease-causing technology and become the vehicle of germ warfare. What this in turn tells us is that, just as no technology, including nuclear weapons, can be so out of human control as to be unremittingly bad, so is no technology so out of our control as to be undilut-edly good. Human direction, whether for good or evil, is decisive in all things technological.

All technologies, then, are one form of knife or another in our hands. This is good news, in that it shows the fallacy of the view that technology is autonomous or intrinsically out of our control. But, of course, it also confers upon us a continuing responsibility to use technology for positive purposes—and to do what we can to remedy a technology that may have negative effects.

In the next section, we consider a low-profile but highly instructive case in point of our capacity to exercise this responsibility: the window and its sundry coverings.

The Parable of the Window Shade

Once upon a time, people were obliged to suffer wind and rain in their faces if they wanted a glimpse of the outside world from within their abodes on a nasty day: They had to look through small holes in their walls. The window was a wonderful remedy for these circumstances, in that it allowed people to see the outside, but through a pane of glass that protected them from the elements.

As often happens in technological evolution, however, the window created a new problem even as it solved the old one: for while residents could easily look out, other people could easily look in. The window and its safe permeability to the outside, in other words, also brought into being the Peeping Tom.

Here we have a classic case of a technological benefit engendering a disadvantage—in this case, an unexpected loss of privacy.

The human response to this new problem is instructive: We invented curtains, venetian blinds, window shades, and the like. Rather than passively suffer the Peeping Tom, we created new technologies that both preserved the benefits of the original window and eliminated the new problem it had brought into being.

Indeed, the development of what I call "remedial media" is a fundamental pattern in technological development and has played a role in many threads of its evolution. Television, to take another kind of window as an example, was criticized in its first twenty-five years for being an extremely ephemeral medium—providing no sense of past or future, just the present, to its viewers. Lewis Mumford, in his *Pentagon of Power* (1970), went so far as to say that such unremitting immediacy was akin to a brain-damaged state for humans. But, as we have seen above, nothing in technology is utterly unremitting. And thus, even as Mumford was making this criticism, videotaping devices were being developed that would soon give television a memory—and a sense of future as well—as people could record programs for re-viewing and/or set their videocassette recorders (VCRs) to tape a future program. The VCR thus is television's window shade: It allows viewers the benefits of TV while reducing the powerlessness that formerly characterized its viewing. It turned television, at least on the question of viewer control, into something more like a book.

So remedial media gives substance to the logical claim that humans have continuing control over our technologies. But some critics contend that the very prevalence of technology in our world is the problem—so that the introduction of any new technology, even a remedial one, is ipso facto not to our benefit. [One] technological effect often cited in such concerns [is] information overload, or the view that we are drowning in the options our technology offers. . . .

In the next section, we'll see how [this] concern is based on profound misunderstandings of the technological process—and how, in fact, the introduction of new technologies serves to help the very problems that critics claim are engendered by technology.

OVERLOAD AS UNDERLOAD

Information is undeniably essential to life, and therein even more so to human life. Are critics right that we can have too much of a good thing?

It is useful to point out in such a context that, socially, tragedies commonly arise from misunderstandings based on too little, not too much, information. The Battle of New Orleans, one of many examples that can be plucked from history, was fought *after* the treaty ending the War of 1812 between the United States and England had been signed in Paris. Why was this? It was because news of the treaty's signing was making its way to the New World by boat. The Battle of New Orleans was thus a direct effect of insufficient, or in this case, simply missing, information: The invention of the telegraph some twenty years later would have prevented this battle from ever occurring.

But what of the claim that the sum total of information has increased so greatly in the past two centuries that the balance has shifted from too little to too much? Here we need to look a little more closely at how human cognition processes information—for to say that we have too much information is to be saying, in effect, that our brains have limitations on how much information they can handle, and these limitations have already been reached.

THE INFORMATION SUPERHIGHWAY

The Information Superhighway is more than the Internet. It is a series of components, including the collection of public and private high-speed, interactive, narrow, and broadband networks that exist today and will emerge tomorrow.

- It is the satellite, terrestrial, and wireless technologies that deliver content to homes, businesses, and other public and private institutions.

- It is the information and content that flow over the infrastructure, whether in the form of databases, the written word, a film, a piece of music, a sound recording, a picture, or computer software.

- It is the computers, televisions, telephones, radios, and other products that people will employ to access the infrastructure.

- It is the people who will provide, manage, and generate new information, and those who will help others to do the same.

- And it is the individual Americans who will use and benefit from the Information Superhighway.

A Nation of Opportunity: A Final Report of the United States Advisory Council on the National Information Infrastructure, January 1996.

We can begin by recognizing that our brains are not mere passive buckets, into which the experience of the world is deposited until it reaches a certain "full" point beyond which, like water in a pail, it overflows. Much to the contrary, as philosophers and psychologists from Immanuel Kant to John Dewey to Jean Piaget have recognized, our cognition is a highly active digesting agent—rather than merely absorbing information, we process it as it comes in to us, changing it in the processing, categorizing it, shaping it, linking it to other information at all steps so that the end result is both more complex and unified than the raw ingredients with which this activity of understanding began. While there may not be any reason to assume this processing is somehow ultimately immune from all possible overflow, neither can this Kantian active view of the mind support a model that has our mentality simply overwhelmed by too great a quantity of information. The mind just doesn't work like that.

Indeed, contrary to popular impressions of late twentieth-century society as being overwhelmed with information, the actual evidence suggests that our mentalities are dealing quite well with the big, booming, buzzing world of confusion identified by William James more than a century ago as the proper pool from which our consciousness selects candidates for its attention. We daily walk into bookstores and libraries, stocked by packets of information—books—on a magnitude thousands of times more than we can possibly read. And although we may well feel a little pressured or momentarily baffled as we would in any large, crowded environment, we rarely feel the kind of acute, overwhelming anxiety associated with overload that paralyzes or disrupts our ability to respond or act. We instead usually make our selections from the huge array quite effectively and comfortably in the end.

Navigating Bookstores and the Internet

Why would bookstores and libraries not be loci of information overload, in presumed contrast to computers and their output, which are the usual suspects in current overload castigations? A closer scrutiny reveals that we have, not surprisingly, developed navigational techniques for processing the high informational invitation of bookstores and libraries. Every child learns in school that books can be meaningfully organized according to subject and author. Special cases are accorded special, rationally coherent treatment. Biographies, for example, are usually shelved in alphabetical order of neither the title nor author, but the subject's last name. Paperbacks may be put in special sections regardless of their subject, and so forth. The result is a complex system—a remedial medium for the bookstore and library, to use the parlance introduced above—that is internalized by most literate people well before attaining adulthood.

And this in turn suggests that what may be vexing about current computer networks—the Web, the Internet, and the enormous access to information they provide—is not that they give us too much information, but that we have too little information, *navigational* information to be more exact, with which to adequately process these new sources of knowledge. Indeed, when we consider that we have had more than five hundred years to devise effective navigational strategies for the printing press's output, and little more than five years to learn to navigate a burgeoning worldwide Internet, our feeling of being overwhelmed is quite understandable.

MORE TECHNOLOGY IS NEEDED

But it is, on the basis of the above development of navigational procedures for books, quite transitory. Characteristically, critics of technology who have simply attacked the problem as access to too much information, with the implicit or explicit call for a reduction of technology, have made the problem only worse. For if this information overload is really underload—a problem that arises from too little, not too much, informational technology—then the call for a reduction of technology cuts precisely in the wrong direction. What is needed is *more* technology— enough social and technical structure to support our cognitive capacities in this new realm.

Indeed, new technologies that are daily becoming more available are already providing some of the wherewithal to deal with the huge amounts of information they offer. Active processing of information by the mind is the natural antidote to overload, as we have seen, and personal computers connected to on-line systems via telephone lines turn out to be opening not only enormous gateways for receipt of information, but easy means for insertion of information by users back into the system—allowing for contribution of information, which is the most active type of information processing of all. Indeed, unlike television and books and all mass media before it, on-line communication allows for a dialogue in which readers become authors. And the process of reading a text of which you are in part an author, in which some part of what you read is a response to your words, instantly gives you an inside understanding of the information, puts you on top of rather than underneath the mass of data it may engender.

PERIODICAL BIBLIOGRAPHY

The following articles have been selected to supplement the diverse views presented in this chapter. Addresses are provided for periodicals not indexed in the *Readers' Guide to Periodical Literature*, the *Alternative Press Index*, the *Social Sciences Index*, or the *Index to Legal Periodicals and Books*.

Chip Bayers	"The Great Web Wipeout," *Time*, January 27, 1997.
Ulrich Beck	"Freedom for Technology," *Dissent*, Fall 1995.
Steve Case	"On-Line Service: Information and Communication," *Vital Speeches of the Day*, May 15, 1996.
Esther Dyson et al.	"A Magna Carta for the Knowledge Age," *New Perspectives Quarterly*, Fall 1994.
Joseph Epstein	"An Extremely Well-Informed SOB," *American Scholar*, Winter 1995.
James Fallows	"Caught in the Web," *New York Review of Books*, February 15, 1996.
Bill Gates	"A View from Olympus," *Forbes ASAP*, December 2, 1996.
William Gibson	"The Net Is a Waste of Time," *New York Times Magazine*, July 14, 1996.
Andrew Grove	"What Can Be Done, Will Be Done," *Forbes ASAP*, December 2, 1996.
Raymond Lane	"The Information Age Is Not Yet Here," *New Perspectives Quarterly*, Spring 1997.
Patrick McCormick	"Are We Just Shark Bait in a Sea of Information?" *U.S. Catholic*, January 1997.
Richard H. Nethe	"Mixed Blessings: Second Thoughts on the Information Explosion," *Humanist*, September/October 1996.
Richard John Neuhaus	"The Internet Produces a Global Village of Village Idiots," *Forbes ASAP*, December 2, 1996.

Kirkpatrick Sale et al.   "Information Technology: Boon or Bane?"
Futurist, January/February 1997.

Joe Schultz   "Evolution, Revolution, or Reformation?"
Macworld, October 1996.

David Shenk   "Data Smog: Surviving the Info Glut,"
Technology Review, May/June 1997.

Jennifer Tanaka   "Drowning in Data," Newsweek, April 28, 1997.

Frederick Turner   "Less Freedom. Slower Speed. More Blockages.
(. . . Just What the Internet Needs.)," American
Enterprise, March/April 1996.

WILL THE INFORMATION REVOLUTION TRANSFORM EDUCATION?

CHAPTER PREFACE

In the early 1990s, Arthur Andersen, an information resources organization, initiated a project entitled "School of the Future." Its goal is to develop a new education system that fosters active study, creativity, critical thinking, and the desire for lifelong learning. To this end, Arthur Andersen contributed an experimental "learning environment" to a public high school. The learning environment is a new kind of classroom: Instead of rows of desks rigidly lined up to face the teacher, the room is composed of islandlike installations that include networked computers with Internet access and CD-ROM capabilities, computer simulation tools, and other research-enhancing technologies. Students work on specified projects in small groups, comparing ideas, accessing information, analyzing data, and preparing reports. Teachers work as facilitators rather than lecturers, counseling individual students, preparing future curricula, and occasionally leading provocative discussions on topics related to student projects. Supporters of the high-tech learning environment contend that it will enhance students' curiosity and creativity, foster teamwork, and prepare students for work in an information-age workplace. According to Richard L. Measelle, managing partner of Arthur Andersen, "Our results to date are very encouraging. . . . By learning how to access new information, [students] have gained the ability to create their own knowledge, rather than simply memorizing knowledge in bits and pieces. They still learn specifics; but they have also learned how to learn them."

Some educators, however, are skeptical about increasing the use of computers in the classroom. David Gelernter, professor of computer science at Yale University, argues that what schools need to emphasize is basic reading, writing, and math skills—not Internet access or high-tech classrooms. He contends that "our children are barely able to handle the data they already have—the databases and computer CDs and videotapes at many public libraries, the newspapers they don't read, the 24-hour news channels and C-SPANs they don't watch, the old-fashioned books they ignore. Couldn't we teach them to use what they've got before favoring them with three orders of magnitude more?" Gelernter and other educators maintain, furthermore, that the computer's natural speed discourages the slow, careful thought and focused attention required for in-depth intellectual analysis.

The authors in the following chapter offer additional commentary on the information revolution's effect on education.

"This postindustrial form of society calls for a new, postindustrial form of education."

THE INFORMATION REVOLUTION WILL TRANSFORM EDUCATION

National Academy of Sciences

The National Academy of Sciences is a private organization founded by the U.S. Congress to advise the federal government on scientific and technical matters. In the following viewpoint, the academy argues that schools must change in order to prepare students for the workplace of the future. The information revolution is transforming the work world and will require future workers to be flexible and to have updated skills and knowledge, the academy contends. Therefore, they conclude, schools must use technological innovations to teach students how to work cooperatively in gathering, analyzing, and utilizing information.

As you read, consider the following questions:

1. How do the authors describe the "factory school model"?
2. According to the authors, in what ways can computers be used as effective learning machines?
3. What is the role for teachers under the new model of education, in the authors' view?

Reprinted from *Reinventing Schools: The Technology Is Now!*, an on-line book by the National Academy of Sciences, 1995, at www.nap.edu/readingroom/books/techgap/welcome.html, by permission of the National Academy Press.

Schools tend to reflect the societies in which they are embedded. In America before the Civil War, little book learning was needed to manage what was for most people still an agrarian life. School started relatively late in the day and ended early to leave time for chores. In summer, school let out entirely so children could help their parents in the fields. Education was narrow in scope, controlled largely by the teacher, and focused predominantly on basic skills.

In that world, the model of education embodied in the one-room schoolhouse was sufficient. Teachers taught reading, writing, and elementary mathematics to complement the skills students learned outside school. Since relatively few students progressed even as far as high school, the need for higher levels of education was minimal.

OUTDATED MODELS OF EDUCATION

By the end of the 19th century, more and more of the population was settling in cities and going to work in factories. To teach students the basic skills and simple facts they needed for industrial jobs, the first great revolution in schooling took place: the factory school model appeared. Large buildings enclosed labyrinths of classrooms where students sat in neat rows with the teacher in front. Schools sought to be an efficient social institution that could turn out identical products. Students learned enough to work at jobs that they would probably keep for much of their lives.

Today many students still attend factory-model schools. Much of the day is spent passively listening to lectures. Many classes teach skills for jobs that either no longer exist or will not exist in their present form when students grow up.

It is clear that yesterday's innovation has become today's obstacle to change. Only about 20 percent of the employed population now works in factories or on farms. People graduating from high school or college will average six to eight jobs over the course of a career, many of them requiring skills that are unforeseen today. About half of all employed Americans work with information—analyzing information that already exists, generating new information, storing and retrieving information. Soon a major portion of this group will not even work in an office, much less a factory, but at home.

This postindustrial form of society calls for a new, postindustrial form of education. Teachers, parents, school administrators, and policymakers have begun to realize that an entirely new model of education is needed. In this new kind of school, all students will be held to far higher standards of learning because everyone will have to be prepared to think for a living and everyone will have to be capable of learning many new skills over the course of a lifetime. This model of education will increase the links between students and their communities, bringing the resources of school to bear on the complex ethical, civic, and technical decisions that all citizens will have to make. The timing and location of education will be more flexible, to reflect and take advantage of changes in the workplace. The distinction between learning inside of school and outside of school will blur.

Technology is a key transforming element in creating this new model of school. Just as technology is reshaping other institutions, it has the potential to reshape education, ending the disjunction between school and the broader society. Technology offers unlimited new ways of learning, of teaching, and of running schools. It provides new ways for everyone involved in education to be openly accountable to parents, to communities, and to students.

TECHNOLOGY AND THE NEW MODEL OF LEARNING AND TEACHING

Yet technology by itself is clearly not enough. As applied in factory-model schools, technology can be as uninspiring as traditional mimeographed worksheets. Computers in schools have too often been used for drills, for word processing, and for remedial work. These applications fail to take advantage of the rich, interactive capabilities of today's information technologies.

Compare the use of computers for drill and practice to their use as effective learning machines. With imaginative, inspiring software, students are not forced to come up with the one right answer; rather, they learn to ask many questions and to devise multiple approaches to a problem. They learn at their own pace and in their own style, so that skilled students advance without restraint while other students have the various resources they need to meet high standards.

Traditional schools have emphasized individual performance and competition and have discouraged students from working or even talking together. In the new model of school, classroom experiences emphasize critical thinking, teamwork, compromise, and communication—the skills valued in today's workplace.

This model of education calls for changing the roles of students, teachers, and schools. In the new model of school, students assume many of the functions previously reserved for teachers. In small groups, individual students act as peer-tutors for others. Because they are often the ones most familiar with new technologies, students lead by example, helping their classmates work through problems. In this way, students begin learning from an early age how to communicate and how to assume greater responsibility for their own education.

THE SCHOOL OF THE FUTURE

Our work [on the "School of the Future"] has confirmed several guiding principles.

• First of all, passive learning is passé. Students must become self-directed learners. This means creating a school environment that will engage students in "discovery" learning—exploring new knowledge for themselves, the very same way they learned naturally, before starting school.

• Teachers, too, must be transformed—from lecturers who impart facts to facilitators who offer tools and advice to young learners.

• Students should be equipped to learn in their own unique style and at their own pace. They should move ahead as they demonstrate actual mastery . . . not just to stay in step with their classmates, for the convenience of administrators. . . .

• We should actively encourage students to learn cooperation. This can be done partly by creating multi-age groupings that enable more experienced students to help others learn. We should actively foster teamwork as both a learning technique and a link to today's modern, cooperative workplace.

• We can also reinforce this link to the workplace by taking full advantage of computer technology's potential to create simulated real-life situations. Our experience shows that becoming engaged with these situations will interest and challenge students much more than any one discipline can do by itself.

Richard L. Measelle, *Vital Speeches of the Day*, June 1, 1996.

Teachers, in contrast, change from being the repository of all knowledge to being guides or mentors who help students navigate through the information made available by technology and interactive communications. They help students gather and organize information, judge its value, and decide how to present it to others. Moving from group to group and from student to student, teachers help students stay focused and working at the limits of their abilities. When the class meets as a whole, teachers share the responsibility for teaching with the students—each of whom has been forging ahead at his or her own pace.

A New Model of Education

In this new model of school, education looks different than it does in most schools today. Schools might be open all day and all year, with groups of students rotating in and out of session. Classrooms might include students of different ages. Traditional 50-minute classes will stretch or disappear to accommodate activities made possible by technology. Longer-term projects will cut across disciplines, combining the subject matter of previously separate classes. Multiple choice tests will be replaced by new kinds of assessments that measure the acquisition of higher-order skills.

Schools may emerge in unlikely places—such as office buildings—or more conventional schools may have branch campuses integrated into businesses, hospitals, or homes. Secondary schools may forge new links with two-year colleges and community institutions to ease the transition from school to work. Individual classes will be integrated into workplaces, providing a vocational education far richer and more useful than what is offered today. Technologies used at home will convey lesson plans, homework, and assessments both to students and to their parents.

The ultimate goal of this new model of education is to foster communities of lifelong learners, where intellect and cooperation are highly valued. Within these communities, decisions will be made by those in the best position to make them—by students, teachers, and educational administrators.

The elements of this new model of education are starting to appear in scattered communities across the United States. Schools are experimenting with new organizational structures, new forms of governance, and new uses of technology that are designed to reflect the constant flux of modern society. This trend is about to accelerate dramatically. As technology becomes more powerful and plentiful, and as the needs of society more urgently call for a new model of education, American schools will be caught up by irresistible forces of change.

*"As a learning device, the new
electronic technology . . . may be
more bad than good."*

THE INFORMATION REVOLUTION
MAY NOT IMPROVE EDUCATION

Gertrude Himmelfarb

As with past communications revolutions—such as print,
movies, and television—the information revolution will have
both good and bad consequences for society and particularly for
education, Gertrude Himmelfarb argues in the following viewpoint. For example, she points out, computer technology is a
boon for research, but the computer's natural speed does not
foster the slow, patient thought required for the comprehension
of complex ideas. She contends that schoolchildren should still
be taught the basic skills of reading, writing, and arithmetic in
order to develop the critical thinking capacity to interpret and
understand the high volume of information that will be produced in the future. Himmelfarb is a professor emeritus of history at the Graduate School and University Center of the City
University of New York.

As you read, consider the following questions:

1. According to Himmelfarb, how did movies, radio, and
   television make inroads on the book?
2. In the author's opinion, what is the drawback of using the
   Internet to retrieve information?
3. In the author's view, what is important in the history of
   ideas?

Reprinted from "A Neo-Luddite Reflects on the Internet," by Gertrude Himmelfarb,
Chronicle of Higher Education, November 1, 1996, by permission of the author.

On the subject of our latest technological revolution, cyber-space, I am a neo-Luddite. Not a true Luddite; my Luddism is qualified, compromised. I revel in the word processor; I am grateful for computerized library catalogues; I appreciate the convenience of CD-ROMs; and I concede the usefulness of the Internet for retrieving information and conducting research. But I am disturbed by some aspects of the new technology—not merely by the moral problems raised by cybersex, which have occupied so much attention recently, but also by the new technology's impact on learning and scholarship.

THE PRINT REVOLUTION'S IMPACT ON CULTURE

Revolutions come fast and furious these days. No sooner do we adapt to one than we are confronted with another. For almost half a millennium, we lived with the product of the print revolution—the culture of the book. Then, a mere century ago, we were introduced to the motion picture; a couple of decades later, to radio and then to television. To a true Luddite, those inventions were the beginning of the rot, the decline of Western civilization as we have known it. To a true revolutionary, such as Marshall McLuhan, they were giant steps toward a brave new world liberated from the stultifying rigidities of an obsolete literacy. To the rest of us, they were frivolities, diversions, often meretricious (as some popular culture has always been), but not threatening to the life of the mind, the culture associated with books.

Not that the book culture has been immune from corruption. When the printing press democratized literature, liberating it from the control of clerics and scribes, the effects were ambiguous. As the historian Elizabeth Eisenstein pointed out in her seminal 1979 work *The Printing Press as an Agent of Change*, the advent of printing facilitated not only the production of scientific works, but also of occult and devotional tracts. It helped create a cosmopolitan secular culture and, at the same time, distinctive national and sectarian cultures. It stimulated scholarship and high culture, as well as ephemera and popular culture. It subverted one intellectual elite, the clergy, only to elevate another, the "enlightened" class.

Yet for all of its ambiguities, printing celebrated the culture of the book—of bad books, to be sure, but also of good books and great books. Movies, radio, and television made the first inroads on the book, not only because they distracted us from reading, but also because they began to train our minds to respond to oral and visual sensations of brief duration rather than to the cadences, nuances, and lingering echoes of the written word. The movie critic Michael Medved has said that even more detrimental than the content of television is the way that it habituates children to an attention span measured in seconds rather than minutes. The combination of sound bites and striking visual effects shapes the young mind, incapacitating it for the longer, slower, less febrile tempo of the book.

And now we have the Internet to stimulate and quicken our senses still more. We channel-surf on television, but that is naught compared with cyber-surfing. The obvious advantage of the new medium is that it provides access to an infinite quantity of information on an untold number and variety of subjects. How does one quarrel with such a plenitude of goods?

THE RELIABILITY OF INFORMATION ON THE INTERNET

As an information-retrieval device, the Internet is unquestionably an asset, assuming that those using it understand that the information retrieved is only as sound as the original sources—an assumption that applies to all retrieval methods, but especially to one whose sources are so profuse and indiscriminate. Yet children and even older students, encouraged to rely upon the Internet for information and research, may not be sophisticated enough to question the validity of the information or the reliability of the source. A child whom I saw interviewed on television said that it was wonderful to be able to ask a question on one's home page and have "lots of people answer it for you." Before the age of the Internet, the child would have had to look up the question in a textbook or encyclopedia, sources that he would have recognized as more authoritative than, say, his older brother or sister (or even his mother or father).

As a learning device, the new electronic technology is even more dubious—indeed, it may be more bad than good. And it is dubious at all levels of learning. Children who are told that they need not learn how to multiply and divide, spell, and write grammatical prose, because the computer can do that for them, are being grossly miseducated. More important, young people constantly exposed to "multimedia" and "hypermedia" replete with sound and images often become unable to concentrate on mere "texts" (known as books), which only have words and ideas to commend them. Worse yet, the constant exposure to a myriad of texts, sounds, and images that often are only tangentially related to each other is hardly conducive to the cultivation of logical, rational, systematic habits of thought.

At the more advanced level of learning and scholarship, the situation is equally ambiguous. Let me illustrate this from my own experience. I used to give (in the pre-electronic age) two sequences of courses: one on social history, the other on intellectual history. In a course on social history, a student might find electronic technology useful, for example, in inquiring about the standard of living of the working classes in the early period of industrialization, assuming that the relevant sources—statistical surveys, diaries, archival collections, newspapers, tracts, journals, books, and other relevant materials—were on line (or at least that information about their location and content was available).

INFORMATION HIGHWAY ROADKILL.

©1994 P.S. Mueller. Reprinted with permission.

This kind of social history, which is built by marshaling social and economic data, is not only facilitated, but actually is stimulated, by the new technology. One might find oneself making connections among sources of information that would have had no apparent link had they not been so readily called up on the computer screen (on the other hand, now one might not make the effort to discover other kinds of sources that do not appear).

The Drawbacks of Reading Books on the Screen

But what about intellectual history? It may be that the whole of [Jean-Jacques] Rousseau's *Social Contract* and [Georg Wilhelm Friedrich] Hegel's *Philosophy of History* are now on line. Can one read such books on the screen as they should be read—slowly, carefully, patiently, dwelling upon a difficult passage, resisting the temptation to scroll down, thwarting the natural speed of the computer? What is important in the history of ideas is not retrieving and recombining material, but understanding it. And that requires a different relation to the text, a different tempo of reading and study.

One can still buy the book (or perhaps print out a "hard copy" from the computer), read it, mark it up, and take notes the old-fashioned way. The difficulty is that students habituated to surfing on the Internet, to getting their information in quick, easy doses, to satisfying their curiosity with a minimum of effort (and with a maximum of sensory stimulation) often do not have the patience to think and study this old-fashioned way. They may even come to belittle the intellectual enterprise itself, the study of the kinds of books—"great books," as some say derisively—that require careful thought and study.

Perhaps I am exaggerating the effect of the electronic revolution, just as critics have said that Elizabeth Eisenstein has exaggerated the effect of the print one. She sometimes seems to suggest that printing was not only *an* agent of change, but *the* primary agent. Without the printing press, she has implied, the Renaissance might have petered out or the Reformation been suppressed as yet another medieval heresy. "The advent of printing," she notes, preceded "the Protestant revolt."

THE ELECTRONIC REVOLUTION AND INTELLECTUAL DEVELOPMENT

The electronic media cannot make that claim to priority. The intellectual revolution of our time, postmodernism, long antedated the Internet. Nonetheless, the Internet powerfully reinforces postmodernism: It is the postmodernist technology *par excellence*. It is as subversive of "linear," "logocentric," "essentialist" thinking, as committed to the "aporia," "indeterminacy," "fluidity," "intertextuality," and "contextuality" of discourse, as deconstruction itself. Like postmodernism, the Internet does not distinguish between the true and the false, the important and the trivial, the enduring and the ephemeral. The search for a name or phrase or subject will produce a comic strip or advertising slogan as readily as a quotation from the Bible or Shakespeare. Every source appearing on the screen has the same weight and credibility as every other; no authority is "privileged" over any other.

The Internet gives new meaning to the British expression describing intellectuals, "chattering classes." On their own home pages, subscribers can communicate to the world every passing reflection, impression, sensation, obsession, or perversion.

Michael Kinsley, editor of the new cyberspace journal *Slate*, defensively insists that his magazine will retain the "linear, ratio-nal thinking" of print journalism. To have to make that claim is itself testimony to the non-linear, non-rational tendency of the new medium. Each article in *Slate* gives the date when it was "posted" and "composted" (archived). Composted! One recalls the computer-programming acronym a few years ago—"GIGO," for "garbage in, garbage out." (As it happens, the articles in *Slate* are not garbage, but much on the Internet is.)

One need not be a Luddite, or even a neo-Luddite, to be alarmed by this most useful, most potent, most seductive, and most equivocal invention.

| "Computer systems in schools should be viewed as structured learning environments with complex and comprehensive capabilities to access and manipulate information."

SCHOOLS SHOULD EMPHASIZE COMPUTER EDUCATION

Chris Morton

In the following viewpoint, Chris Morton argues that computers are not used effectively in education. Schools too often train students to simply use computers as tools, he argues, preparing them for traditional jobs and industries that may not exist in the future. Computer technology should instead be used as a learning environment in which students collect, interpret, and communicate information, he maintains. Such computer-based education, Morton contends, would give students the skills they will need for the workplace of the future. Morton is president of the International Institute for Information Analysis in Yorktown Heights, New York.

As you read, consider the following questions:

1. In Morton's opinion, how are schools today similar to Jonathan Swift's fictional island of Laputa?
2. According to the author, how does the concept of "computer-as-tool" lead to the rejection of computer systems in schools?
3. Which educational approaches does Morton contend educational planners have largely ignored?

Reprinted from "The Modern Land of Laputa: Where Computers Are Used in Education," by Chris Morton, Phi Delta Kappan, February 1996, by permission of the author and the Phi Delta Kappan.

In the 17th century, satirist Jonathan Swift described his hero, Gulliver, visiting a flying island where science and technology were primary functions. One would expect this land to be a very modern and progressive place. But Laputa turned out to be a limited place where nothing was ever accomplished, because its people, deaf to change, reveled in following the same ludicrous procedures over and over again. With minimal rewriting, this satire might well describe many schools today and their use of technology.

In the 1970s schools crippled the first stage in the educational use of computers by insisting that teachers learn BASIC as an introduction to technology use in classrooms. The teachers returned to their schools to find that they had no use for their training and, as is almost always the case, no time for reflecting on or developing new directions for using technology. Disillusionment quickly set in.

In the 1980s and 1990s we continue to destroy the foundation that would allow the development of educational uses of computers by defining the technological infrastructure in ways that discredit it, that mislead planners, and that provide ready ammunition for those who oppose such uses of technology. The new rush to fund computer systems through bond issues does nothing to alleviate the situation. Indeed, it may soon exacerbate the problems. It is time to take stock of these expanding mistakes, which are being perpetrated primarily by poorly trained educational administrators, particularly school superintendents.

COMPUTERS AS "TOOLS"

The April 1987 issue of *School Administrator*, the official organ of the American Association of School Administrators, featured on its cover a computer and a pencil, as if the one were an extension of the other. Inside, the editorial confirmed this perception, and the "official" misconception of "computer as tool" was born, at least for administrators.

The concept of "computer as tool" misleads educational planners and relegates computer technology to the level of "supplies"—pencils, paper, pens, and paper clips. Because of this definition, school business managers and educational planners (particularly curriculum planners) conceptually align computers with traditional classroom "tools" that can be used as "alternatives." This view leads them to put computers on a cost continuum with pens and pencils and allows decision makers to reject computers as "expensive alternatives" to things we already use.

But that's not all. The concept of "computer as tool" allows the uninformed to make easy decisions about the use of computers in schools. It allows administrators and teachers to reject the computer as simply one "tool" among many, without having to understand what its capabilities for learning and productivity really are. The idea of "computer as tool" permits the ignorant to justify their decision to reject it.

Human beings were initially distinguished from other animals as "tool users." When anthropologists noted that many wild animals use tools, they changed the definition to "tool makers." However, once it was discovered that some wild animals make tools (e.g., chimpanzees strip twigs to dip insects out of their nests), humans became the "information gatherers and storers."

To suggest, therefore, that computers are simply tools entirely misses the point about their expanding capabilities and their interaction with humans. In the larger society, the computer is a symbol of the future and all that is good about it. We should not be surprised that educators would want to update their largely 19th-century practice by using computers as tools to support their efforts. But while the real world uses computers to move forward, educators too often look studiously backward, and Laputa is reborn.

Computer systems in schools should be viewed as structured learning environments with complex and comprehensive capabilities to access and manipulate information. They should be seen as interactive learning extensions of the children themselves.

We live in a society in which the technological environment is an accepted part of our lives. It is only in schools that we consider the computer to be an add-on, a thing little related to skills development or communications.

COMPUTERS AS ADD-ONS

The stereotype of the "computer as tool" promotes the view of the "computer as add-on." But the "add-on" concept goes a lot deeper; it allows curriculum developers to continue implementing their traditionally fragmented, subject-based, single-discipline-focused instructional plans, rather than regarding and using the computer as the driving force behind an integrated, cross-disciplinary learning environment that emulates the "real" world. Computer technology provides learning environments that promote individual attainment, group interaction and sharing, a choice of various approaches to a particular project, and access to current information.

Curriculum development and training are traditionally considered to be at the core of instructional development and the integration of learning models. This is a Laputian truism that is repeated again and again. What it leads to is a glacial system whose movement is frozen. Curriculum change takes most schools and education departments many years to implement and sometimes produces hilarious situations, such as a 10th-grade curriculum called "Global Studies" whose 10-year-old content and textbooks still refer to Russia as part of the U.S.S.R. The exclusion of computer technology from the processes of planning, managing, and implementing curriculum and instruction keeps change in education moving at a snail's pace and maintains the old instructional models.

ATTRACTING LEARNERS' ATTENTION

[One] feature of the World Wide Web worth noting here is its multimedia capability. This is more than a gimmick, although in many current uses the addition of sound, graphics, video, etc., to Web pages adds little of substance. Eventually, however, as developers become more comfortable with the integration of multiple sources and forms of information, the Web will have wide-ranging consequences for how people communicate, access and remember information, and occupy new zones of experience that span ordinary distinctions of "learning" and "entertainment."

Educators in schools are going to have to become a great deal more creative and ingenious in finding educational experiences that can attract the attention and interest of learners whose tastes and expectations are being shaped by these new digital environments. The educational community will have to compete even more with alternative communities of affiliation.

Nicholas C. Burbules, *Education Digest*, May 1997.

Because the computer environment has the potential to stimulate learning, because it is pervasive in society, because computer-based skills must be taught to children, because of the speed at which the computer can support change, and because of the expanded vision that the computer gives to students and teachers, it is difficult to understand why curriculum planners exclude computer-based learning environments from curriculum development. Instead of being integral to curriculum development and completely integrated into it, the computer environment remains peripheral, an "add-on" in space and time that many teachers and administrators can reject.

This "add-on" is often provided in laboratory settings, where scheduled periods allow students to "do" computing. In such settings everything positive and creative about the computer environment is destroyed. Moreover, individual teachers who would like to embrace a computerized learning environment are forced by these arrangements to compete with other teachers for access to these sporadically used "tools."

The worst-case scenario (usually in late middle school or early high school) typically involves students' going through a process of acquiring "computer literacy" by sitting in rows and being exposed a couple of times a week to those "tool skills"—such as word processing, keyboarding, and spreadsheet use—which are thought to be important for them to master at some point in their school careers. In these settings students do not learn that the computer environment is all-embracing, that it provides enormous opportunities for learning, and that it can encourage student engagement and access to the "real world." In these settings teachers are not able to realize the instructional potential of the computer systems they control.

When the computer is viewed as "add-on," student learning is as regimented and boring as it has ever been in a one-desk-behind-another environment. The real discouragement of learning in these settings is that they pander to 19th-century didacticism and never come to grips with the genuine benefits of a future-directed computer-based environment with a new skills base.

COMPUTERS AS PART OF THE SAME OLD GAME

In 1989–90 a survey of superintendents in New York and Rhode Island, conducted by the Division of Information Research and Development of the Putnam/North Westchester Board of Cooperative Educational Services, showed that 85% of them knew nothing about computers, had never used a computer, and did not intend to use one. Ninety-five percent of the superintendents knew nothing about educational computing and were not prepared to do anything about this lack of knowledge. And yet these are the people who make decisions about student and teacher uses of computers in schools. While times may have changed to some degree, it doesn't seem likely that all these folks have had significant changes of heart, and there is no reason to believe that the statistics would be any different had the survey been conducted nationally. As Jean Zlotkin, a school board member, says, "It is disastrous to empower unqualified people with critical decision-making power."

In the same years a national survey of 500 universities was conducted to find out whether they included computer training of any sort in their courses for educational administrators. Just

2% of the colleges surveyed said that they provided regular courses for their trainees, 14% said that they offered training through another department, and the rest offered nothing. None of them provided computer-based curriculum training, and only 7% said that their professors used computers in their courses. Yet these institutions are supposed to train school administrators to develop schooling for our children—schooling that prepares them for the twenty-first century. Again, time has passed, and computers have proliferated, but 1989–90 was not exactly the Dark Ages.

It is not surprising, therefore, to find that school administrators balk at the development of computer use in their schools and misdirect planning for it. It is not surprising that, when financial problems plague schools, computing is one of the first areas to suffer cuts. It is not surprising that, when new experimental computer-based programs are introduced into schools, they are treated in the same way as other pilot programs: three years to complete and integrate into the curriculum, with annually declining financing. Of course, we are told that in industry 18 months is the projected desk life of a computer. New computer-based programs require at least a four-year implementation period, with *increasing* funding, if they are to attain the planned goals and to be upgraded as necessary. Given all these facts, it is hardly surprising that, when schools begin to look at change and to focus on student-based outcomes, computer environments are not considered integral to this planning.

EDUCATIONAL POLICY DEVELOPMENT

With regard to educational policy development, funding, and change, it is well to keep in mind that almost all of a state education department's staff is made up of educational administrators. Their lack of a clear focus on computer technology has been demonstrated on numerous occasions. A few examples suffice:

• California cut its most innovative intracurricular computer program in 1991. The program focused on technology integration into classrooms with trained support teams.

• New York has split up the responsibility for computer-use development so that nobody knows what to do. The state has spent millions of dollars on regional training centers that have been in place for 10 years and have produced no measurable change in instruction or computer skills development. Moreover, the state has augmented all of this effort with an out-of-date telecommunications system that nobody wants.

• Massachusetts has recently begun to develop a plan for its schools, after having left such planning to local authorities for the last 15 years.

• Utah has given the responsibility for K–12 computer technology planning to a university-based group; the same group is also responsible for training educational administrators.

Time and again, opportunities have been lost at the state level because of local squabbling, because of a lack of real educational leadership, and because of misleading direction from the federal government.

Computer Environments and Budgeting

It is always important to talk about school budgets. School district budgets in most parts of the country are under fire. They suffered from the recession, and many continue to suffer. Computer environments change often and change comprehensively, but they change much more quickly than educational authorities and planners are accustomed to. School budgets do not adapt well to this rapid pace of change.

Superintendents and school business officials say that schools cannot hope to keep up with the changes in equipment that are taking place in industry. But this is another misconception. Schools must follow the changes in industry because these changes reflect changes in the skills required of students when they leave school.

The new rush to use bond issues to fund computer systems in schools will cause new problems because administrators and school boards refuse to accept the idea that funding for computer systems (including teacher training, software upgrades, video upgrades, satellite use, and system maintenance) must be part of the annual budget and must be looked on as a necessary expense. Bond issues fund hardware and cabling today, but nothing else. If continued funding is not provided, these new systems paid for with millions of taxpayer dollars will become obsolete within five years or less.

School budgets can accommodate technological change by using "technology-based budgeting." This is a simple concept: school budgets must have a minimum percentage of their total funds allocated to technology maintenance and change every year. This minimum is 3% of the total operating budget. Changes can then be gradual and carefully planned. Educational authorities must simply accept the fact that computer technology has a built-in obsolescence period and must be changed regularly.

Serious mistakes on the part of school administrators in budgeting for technology use in schools have left many districts in disastrous positions. Whole systems have become useless, and replacing them has meant the expenditure of huge amounts of money from single budgets. The process of annual "budget hopping" (leaving an item out one year and picking it up the next year or the year after) cannot continue, because the public will not accept the huge outlays or bond issues every three to five years to replace old equipment and planning structures en masse.

COMPUTERS, RESEARCH, AND SKILLS DEVELOPMENT

Many school district administrators (and school board members, who are usually slightly less knowledgeable than their superintendents about educational computing) are demanding research data that show that computer use enhances academic (or other) achievement. This perspective shows a distinct lack of understanding of the computer learning environment.

Special education has shown a better understanding of the potential of computers. The value of a computer environment is not so much the improvement of students' achievement through computer use as it is the improvement of students' ability to achieve. The difficulty of understanding this crucial difference is exacerbated by the focus on "tool use," which insists that the computer is there to enhance abilities already developed.

If the computer is not to be seen as the means of improving achievement in education, then perhaps it should be seen as an integral part of an environment that is structured to engage students in the learning process. Perhaps it should also be regarded as an essential element in an educational approach that focuses on gathering information (and on learning how to transform it into new knowledge), on the changing role of teacher-as-facilitator, on the involvement of children in experiential learning, and on the expanded world of lifelong learning. Educational planners have overlooked these perspectives almost entirely.

In the development of standards and outcomes, nationally and regionally, there is almost no mention of a supporting environment of computer technology. But the skills that graduating students take with them into the world must be a major focus of any serious effort to reform schools, and such computer-based skills as the ability to access and manipulate current information, the ability to communicate globally, the ability to expand creativity, and the ability to test new knowledge through sharing and rebuilding can only be developed in a supportive computer-based environment.

To look for research that shows that computers have improved student performance is misguided for two reasons:

1) schools are not teaching the skills that computer environments best support, and 2) schools have not recognized the skills that students will need in the future.

COMPUTERS AND NEW TEACHING METHODS

For the most part, computer environments will not drastically improve students' attainment in the traditional content that we adhere to in our current curricula and that we reinforce with our didactic methods. If teachers want students to be able to do repetitive tasks and to be able to use ditto masters, then they shouldn't spend thousands of dollars on systems that support computer-assisted instruction. If teachers want to reinforce their didactic role and their role as information providers, then they should also leave computers alone.

Educational administrators must understand that the promise of computer environments is that they support changes in the educational structure, in instructional processes, and in the development of lifelong learning within the whole population. We all pay lip service to the importance for everyone of changing these features of the American educational landscape. But it takes leaders with guts to pursue these future visions and to develop truly different and innovative learning environments that are integrated into technological environments that serve the whole community. From digital television to voice recognition systems, from personal information managers to the Internet, educational challenges and opportunities are here to stay.

If schools refuse to recognize and work with these challenges and opportunities, then they may well follow many of our outmoded industries into decline. Our schools will become ever more like the Laputian community with its repetitive procedures—but, while Laputa continued to exist in its repetitive ignorance, our schools, like some of our industries, will not.

"There are real dangers . . . in looking to technology to be the savior of education."

SCHOOLS SHOULD NOT EMPHASIZE COMPUTER EDUCATION

Todd Oppenheimer

While technology advocates maintain that computers enhance students' academic achievement, Todd Oppenheimer contends in the following viewpoint that there is no evidence to support this claim. There is a significant danger, according to Oppenheimer, that buying computers forces schools to cut other educational programs—such as music, art, and wood shop—that enhance learning. Schools should strive to teach the essentials of reading, writing, and thinking before they teach students to use computers, he argues. Oppenheimer is associate editor of *Newsweek Interactive* and has won a variety of awards for his writing and investigative reporting.

As you read, consider the following questions:

1. According to the poll cited by Oppenheimer, what subjects do teachers consider to be less important than computer skills?
2. How does the author criticize scientific studies that show that computers promote educational achievement?
3. In the author's opinion, what are young students taught through the use of computers?

Reprinted from "The Computer Delusion," by Todd Oppenheimer, *Atlantic Monthly*, July 1997 (cover story), by permission of the author; ©1997 by Todd Oppenheimer.

In 1922 Thomas Edison predicted that "the motion picture is destined to revolutionize our educational system and . . . in a few years it will supplant largely, if not entirely, the use of text-books." Twenty-three years later, in 1945, William Levenson, the director of the Cleveland public schools' radio station, claimed that "the time may come when a portable radio receiver will be as common in the classroom as is the blackboard." Forty years after that the noted psychologist B.F. Skinner, referring to the first days of his "teaching machines," in the late 1950s and early 1960s, wrote, "I was soon saying that, with the help of teaching machines and programmed instruction, students could learn twice as much in the same time and with the same effort as in a standard classroom." Ten years after Skinner's recollections were published, President Bill Clinton campaigned for "a bridge to the twenty-first century . . . where computers are as much a part of the classroom as blackboards." Clinton was not alone in his enthusiasm for a program estimated to cost somewhere between $40 billion and $100 billion over the next five years. Speaker of the House Newt Gingrich, talking about computers to the Republican National Committee early in 1997, said, "We could do so much to make education available twenty-four hours a day, seven days a week, that people could literally have a whole different attitude toward learning."

UNQUESTIONED CLAIMS FOR TECHNOLOGY IN CLASSROOMS

If history really is repeating itself, the schools are in serious trouble. In *Teachers and Machines: The Classroom Use of Technology Since 1920* (1986), Larry Cuban, a professor of education at Stanford University and a former school superintendent, observed that as successive rounds of new technology failed their promoters' expectations, a pattern emerged. The cycle began with big promises backed by the technology developers' research. In the classroom, however, teachers never really embraced the new tools, and no significant academic improvement occurred. This provoked consistent responses: the problem was money, spokespeople argued, or teacher resistance, or the paralyzing school bureaucracy. Meanwhile, few people questioned the technology advocates' claims. As results continued to lag, the blame was finally laid on the machines. Soon schools were sold on the next generation of technology, and the lucrative cycle started all over again.

Today's technology evangels argue that we've learned our lesson from past mistakes. As in each previous round, they say that when our new hot technology—the computer—is compared with yesterday's, today's is better. "It can do the same things, plus," Richard Riley, the U.S. Secretary of Education, told me.

How much better is it, really?

The promoters of computers in schools again offer prodigious research showing improved academic achievement after using their technology. The research has again come under occasional attack, but this time quite a number of teachers seem to be backing classroom technology. In a poll taken early in 1996 U.S. teachers ranked computer skills and media technology as more "essential" than the study of European history, biology, chemistry, and physics; than dealing with social problems such as drugs and family breakdown; than learning practical job skills; and than reading modern American writers such as Steinbeck and Hemingway or classic ones such as Plato and Shakespeare.

CUTTING CLASSES TO BUY COMPUTERS

In keeping with these views New Jersey cut state aid to a number of school districts in 1996 and then spent $10 million on classroom computers. In Union City, California, a single school district is spending $27 million to buy new gear for a mere eleven schools. The Kittridge Street Elementary School, in Los Angeles, killed its music program to hire a technology coordinator; in Mansfield, Massachusetts, administrators dropped proposed teaching positions in art, music, and physical education, and then spent $333,000 on computers; in one Virginia school the art room was turned into a computer laboratory. (Ironically, a half dozen preliminary studies recently suggested that music and art classes may build the physical size of a child's brain, and its powers for subjects such as language, math, science, and engineering—in one case far more than computer work did.) Meanwhile, months after a New Technology High School opened in Napa, California, where computers sit on every student's desk and all academic classes use computers, some students were complaining of headaches, sore eyes, and wrist pain.

Throughout the country, as spending on technology increases, school book purchases are stagnant. Shop classes, with their tradition of teaching children building skills with wood and metal, have been almost entirely replaced by new "technology education programs." In San Francisco only one public school still offers a full shop program—the lone vocational high school. "We get kids who don't know the difference between a screwdriver and a ball peen hammer," James Dahlman, the school's vocational-department chair, told me recently. "How are they going to make a career choice? Administrators are stuck in this mindset that all kids will go to a four-year college and become a doctor or a lawyer, and that's not true. I know some who went to college, graduated, and then had to go back to technical school to get a job." In 1996 the school superintendent in Great Neck, Long Island, proposed replacing elementary school shop classes with computer classes and training the shop teachers as computer coaches. Rather than being greeted with enthusiasm, the proposal provoked a backlash.

Interestingly, shop classes and field trips are two programs that the National Information Infrastructure Advisory Council, the Clinton Administration's technology task force, suggests reducing in order to shift resources into computers. But are these results what technology promoters really intend? "You need to apply common sense," Esther Dyson, the president of EDventure Holdings and one of the task force's leading school advocates, told me recently. "Shop with a good teacher probably is worth more than computers with a lousy teacher. But if it's a poor program, this may provide a good excuse for cutting it. There will be a lot of trials and errors with this. And I don't know how to prevent those errors."

The issue, perhaps, is the magnitude of the errors. Alan Lesgold, a professor of psychology and the associate director of the Learning Research and Development Center at the University of Pittsburgh, calls the computer an "amplifier," because it encourages both enlightened study practices and thoughtless ones. There's a real risk, though, that the thoughtless practices will dominate, slowly dumbing down huge numbers of tomorrow's adults. As Sherry Turkle, a professor of the sociology of science at the Massachusetts Institute of Technology and a longtime observer of children's use of computers, told me, "The possibilities of using this thing poorly so outweigh the chance of using it well, it makes people like us, who are fundamentally optimistic about computers, very reticent.". . .

INCONCLUSIVE RESEARCH ON COMPUTERS IN EDUCATION

Clinton's vision of computerized classrooms arose partly out of the findings of the presidential task force—thirty-six leaders from industry, education, and several interest groups who have guided the Administration's push to get computers into the schools. The report of the task force, "Connecting K–12 Schools to the Information Superhighway" (produced by the consulting firm McKinsey & Co.), begins by citing numerous studies that have apparently proved that computers enhance student achievement significantly. One "meta-analysis" (a study that reviews other studies—in this case 130 of them) reported that computers had improved performance in "a wide range of subjects, including language arts, math, social studies and science." Another found improved organization and focus in students' writing. A third cited twice the normal gains in math skills. Several schools boasted of greatly improved attendance.

"I DON'T HAVE MY HOMEWORK WITH ME... THE COMPUTER ATE IT!"

Unfortunately, many of these studies are more anecdotal than conclusive. Some, including a giant, oft-cited meta-analysis of 254 studies, lack the necessary scientific controls to make solid conclusions possible. The circumstances are artificial and not easily repeated, results aren't statistically reliable, or, most frequently, the studies did not control for other influences, such as differences between teaching methods. This last factor is critical, because computerized learning inevitably forces teachers to adjust their style—only sometimes for the better. Some studies were industry-funded, and thus tended to publicize mostly positive findings. "The research is set up in a way to find benefits that aren't really there," Edward Miller, a former editor of the *Harvard Education Letter*, says. "Most knowledgeable people agree that most of the research isn't valid. It's so flawed it shouldn't even be called research. Essentially, it's just worthless." Once the faulty studies are weeded out, Miller says, the ones that remain "are inconclusive"—that is, they show no significant change in either direction. Even Esther Dyson admits the studies are undependable. "I don't think those studies amount to much either way," she says. "In this area there is little proof."

Why are solid conclusions so elusive? Look at Apple Computer's "Classrooms of Tomorrow," perhaps the most widely studied effort to teach using computer technology. In the early 1980s Apple shrewdly realized that donating computers to schools might help not only students but also company sales, as Apple's ubiquity in classrooms turned legions of families into Apple loyalists. In 1996, after the *San Jose Mercury News* (published in Apple's Silicon Valley home) ran a series questioning the effectiveness of computers in schools, the paper printed an opinion-page response from Terry Crane, an Apple vice-president. "Instead of isolating students," Crane wrote, "technology actually encouraged them to collaborate more than in traditional classrooms. Students also learned to explore and represent information dynamically and creatively, communicate effectively about complex processes, become independent learners and self-starters and become more socially aware and confident."

"THE FILMSTRIPS OF THE 1990s"

Crane didn't mention that after a decade of effort and the donation of equipment worth more than $25 million to thirteen schools, there is scant evidence of greater student achievement. To be fair, educators on both sides of the computer debate acknowledge that today's tests of student achievement are shockingly crude. They're especially weak in measuring intangibles such as enthusiasm and self-motivation, which do seem evident in Apple's classrooms and other computer-rich schools. In any event, what is fun and what is educational may frequently be at odds. "Computers in classrooms are the filmstrips of the 1990s," Clifford Stoll, the author of *Silicon Snake Oil: Second Thoughts on the Information Highway* (1995), told *The New York Times* in May 1996, recalling his own school days in the 1960s. "We loved them because we didn't have to think for an hour, teachers loved them because they didn't have to teach, and parents loved them because it showed their schools were high-tech. But no learning happened."

Stoll somewhat overstates the case—obviously, benefits can come from strengthening a student's motivation. Still, Apple's computers may bear less responsibility for that change than Crane suggests. In the beginning, when Apple did little more than dump computers in classrooms and homes, this produced no real results, according to Jane David, a consultant Apple hired to study its classroom initiative. Apple quickly learned that teachers needed to change their classroom approach to what is commonly called "project-oriented learning." This is an increasingly popular teaching method, in which students learn through doing and teachers act as facilitators or partners rather than as didacts. (Teachers sometimes refer to this approach, which arrived in classrooms before computers did, as being "the guide on the side instead of the sage on the stage.") But what the students learned "had less to do with the computer and more to do with the teaching," David concluded. "If you took the computers out, there would still be good teaching there." This story is heard in school after school, including two impoverished schools—Clear View Elementary School, in southern California, and the Christopher Columbus middle school, in New Jersey—that the Clinton Administration has loudly celebrated for turning themselves around with computers. At Christopher Columbus, in fact, students' test scores rose before computers arrived, not afterward, because of relatively basic changes: longer class periods, new books, after-school programs, and greater emphasis on student projects and collaboration. . . .

JUST A GLAMOROUS TOOL

It would be easy to characterize the battle over computers as merely another chapter in the world's oldest story: humanity's natural resistance to change. But that does an injustice to the forces at work in this transformation. This is not just the future versus the past, uncertainty versus nostalgia; it is about encouraging a fundamental shift in personal priorities—a minimizing of the real, physical world in favor of an unreal "virtual" world. It is about teaching youngsters that exploring what's on a two-dimensional screen is more important than playing with real objects, or sitting down to an attentive conversation with a friend, a parent, or a teacher. By extension, it means downplaying the importance of conversation, of careful listening, and of expressing oneself in person with acuity and individuality. In the process, it may also limit the development of children's imaginations.

Perhaps this is why Steven Jobs, one of the founders of Apple

Computer and a man who claims to have "spearheaded giving away more computer equipment to schools than anybody else on the planet," has come to a grim conclusion: "What's wrong with education cannot be fixed with technology," he told *Wired* magazine in February 1996. "No amount of technology will make a dent. . . . You're not going to solve the problems by putting all knowledge onto CD-ROMs. We can put a Web site in every school—none of this is bad. It's bad only if it lulls us into thinking we're doing something to solve the problem with education." Jane David, the consultant to Apple, concurs, with a commonly heard caveat. "There are real dangers," she told me, "in looking to technology to be the savior of education. But it won't survive without the technology."

Arguments like David's remind Clifford Stoll of yesteryear's promises about television. He wrote in *Silicon Snake Oil,*

> "Sesame Street". . . has been around for twenty years. Indeed, its idea of making learning relevant to all was as widely promoted in the seventies as the Internet is today.

> So where's that demographic wave of creative and brilliant students now entering college? Did kids really need to learn how to watch television? Did we inflate their expectations that learning would always be colorful and fun?

Computer enthusiasts insist that the computer's "interactivity" and multimedia features make this machine far superior to television. Nonetheless, Stoll wrote,

> I see a parallel between the goals of "Sesame Street" and those of children's computing. Both are pervasive, expensive and encourage children to sit still. Both display animated cartoons, gaudy numbers and weird, random noises. . . . Both give the sensation that by merely watching a screen, you can acquire information without work and without discipline.

As the technology critic Neil Postman put it to a Harvard electronic-media conference, "I thought that television would be the last great technology that people would go into with their eyes closed. Now you have the computer."

MAKING FUNDS AVAILABLE FOR BASIC SKILLS

The solution is not to ban computers from classrooms altogether. But it may be to ban federal spending on what is fast becoming an overheated campaign. After all, the private sector, with its constant supply of used computers and the computer industry's vigorous competition for new customers, seems well equipped to handle the situation. In fact, if schools can impose some limits—on technology donors and on themselves—rather than indulging in a consumer frenzy, most will probably find themselves with more electronic gear than they need. That could free the billions that Clinton wants to devote to technology and make it available for impoverished fundamentals: teaching solid skills in reading, thinking, listening, and talking; organizing inventive field trips and other rich hands-on experiences; and, of course, building up the nation's core of knowledgeable, inspiring teachers. These notions are considerably less glamorous than computers are, but their worth is firmly proved through a long history.

In fall 1996, after the school administrators in Mansfield, Massachusetts, had eliminated proposed art, music, and physical-education positions in favor of buying computers, Michael Bellino, an electrical engineer at Boston University's Center for Space Physics, appeared before the Massachusetts Board of Education to protest. "The purpose of the schools [is] to, as one teacher argues, 'Teach carpentry, not hammer,'" he testified. "We need to teach the whys and ways of the world. Tools come and tools go. Teaching our children tools limits their knowledge to these tools and hence limits their futures."

> "We would be wise to ask whether the particularly quaint way in which universities now do their work will survive the transformation of information technology."

THE INFORMATION REVOLUTION WILL TRANSFORM THE UNIVERSITY

William A. Wulf

In the following viewpoint, William A. Wulf argues that universities must adapt themselves to the changes brought about by the information revolution. Because computer networks offer people the ability to do research and communicate with professors from many different locations, he asserts, there is less of a need for students to physically attend a university. Higher education will gain in importance, though, as the information age demands that people engage in a pursuit of lifelong learning. Wulf is the AT&T Professor of Engineering and Applied Science at the University of Virginia in Charlottesville.

As you read, consider the following questions:

1. According to Wulf, in what ways are universities like businesses?
2. In the author's opinion, how can information technology be used to involve students in research and scholarship?
3. How could information technology transform university teaching, according to the author?

Reprinted with permission from *Issues in Science and Technology*, William A. Wulf, "Warning: Information Technology Will Transform the University," Summer 1995, pp. 46–52. Copyright 1995 by the University of Texas at Dallas, Richardson, Texas.

Universities are in the information business, and technological developments are transforming that industry. University professors from a variety of disciplines have helped create the technologies that are forcing many U.S. industries to reinvent themselves, have advised industry leaders on how to adapt, and have analyzed the importance of the changes for society. But it's harder to look inward at the university and to think about whether it might change in dramatic ways. We should remember that although its roots are a millennium old, the university has changed before. In the early 19th century it embraced the notion of secular "liberal" education. In the late 19th century it included scholarship as an integral part of its mission. After World War II it accepted an implied responsibility for national security, economic prosperity, and public health in return for federal funding of research. Although the effects of these changes have been assimilated and now seem "natural," at the time they involved profound reassessment of the mission and structure of the university as an institution.

INFORMATION TECHNOLOGY WILL CHANGE HIGHER EDUCATION

Outside forces are always acting on universities. Some of them, notably the political ones, have great immediacy and hence get a good deal of attention. For example, university administrators are acutely aware of the current reassessment of the rationale for federal funding of research and the desire for greater "productivity" from the faculty, and so on. As important as these changes may be, I believe that information technology has a far greater potential to provoke fundamental change in our system of higher education. Moreover, I am certain that these changes are much closer than most people realize.

Let me be clear. Higher education will flourish. If anything, the need for advanced education is increasing. A greater percentage of the world's population needs to be educated to be productive in an increasingly technological workplace. The period during which particular skills are relevant is shortening, so the need for lifelong learning is growing. The knowledge and skills necessary to function at the frontier of knowledge are expanding as well, increasing the need for advanced degrees.

Higher education is not in danger. But we would be wise to ask whether the particularly quaint way in which universities now do their work will survive the transformation of information technology. It may, but I don't think so. I expect to see major changes—changes not only in the execution of the mission of universities but in our perception of the mission itself.

Traditional Universities Confront Change

Universities historically have changed slowly, but there are times that are more propitious than others for change. The next decade is one such. Because of the speed with which information technology is advancing, decisions are being made now (or more likely, made by default) that will have a material effect on the real and perceived quality of institutions of higher education. In my experience, almost none of the current generation of senior university administrators understand what is happening. They should be confronting two central questions: Are universities like businesses that must adapt to technological change, and is the capability of the technology used for higher education really going to change all that much?

Universities share many of the attributes of traditional handcraft industries. They are highly labor intensive and depend on the skill of their master craftsmen. They have been regional, requiring collocation of the producer and customer, and have contributed to the prestige of their locales. They have a long tradition. They have evolved powerful guilds to protect the masters. And now they face the prospect of a technology that can perform many of the specialized tasks that have made their work valuable.

Universities also share at least some of the attributes of other vertically integrated industries. They "manufacture" information (scholarship) and occasionally "reprocess" it into knowledge or even wisdom, they warehouse it (libraries), they distribute it (articles and books), and they retail it (classroom teaching). Information technology has already changed each of these processes, and future change will be much greater. Like industries that have been overtaken by technology, they need to understand its individual and collective impact on their basic functions. It's not a comfortable thought, but we must at least consider that a change in technology—a change that will facilitate the flow of the university's essential commodity, information—might provoke a change in the nature of the enterprise. . . .

Tapping New Capabilities

How will we use this [information technology] equipment to change education and scholarship? That seems like a simple question, but as both an academic and a computer scientist, I don't know. The ability to process information, the raw stuff of knowledge, sits at the heart of the university mission. A technology that will alter by orders of magnitude our ability to create, store, and communicate knowledge will have an impact on how we fulfill our mission, and possibly on the mission itself. Perhaps as a start we might look at several functions of our vertically integrated information business and note how they have been and might be changed.

The impact of information technology on science is apparent and pervasive. Scientists now routinely talk of computation as the "third modality" of scientific investigation, on a par with theory and experimentation.

| CYBERCOLLEGE

A lot of people have long felt that education is too good to waste on the young, that college should be more than just a rite of passage for Americans. Besides offering the young an alternative means of getting an education, cybercollege is a highly effective means of providing continuing education in a fast-changing world. In 1972 just 28% of U.S. college and university students were over 25. By 1980 the proportion of older students had risen to 34%. In 1994, the last year for which statistics are available, the proportion of older students reached 41%.

The beauty of cyberlearning is that you can pursue it while working at a full-time job and living miles from a college. In an age when many jobs require continuing education, cyberlearning brings it to people who cannot afford to interrupt a career.

Lisa Gubernick and Ashlea Ebeling, *Forbes*, June 16, 1997.

The easy examples are those that simply automate what had been done manually, such as the reduction of data and the control of instruments. The profound applications, however, are those that lead to whole new areas of research and new methods of investigation and thus to science that was not and could not be done before: analyzing molecules that have not been synthesized, measuring the properties of a single neuron by "growing" it on a silicon chip, watching a model of galaxies colliding, and letting a scientist feel the forces as a drug docks in a protein. These applications have transformed the nature of scientific investigation; they have led to questions that would not even have been asked before.

Science, however, will not be where we see the most dramatic impact. I say that despite a recent study (in which I participated) by the National Research Council that paints an expansive image of the transformation of scientific research. I believe that a more dramatic transformation is about to shake the foundations of scholarship in the liberal arts. Humanists will lead the way to innovative applications of the information technology in the university.

The comfortable stereotype of humanists as technophobic is no longer accurate. The availability of text and images in electronic form, coupled with the processing power of modern computers, allow the humanist to explore hypotheses and visualize relations that were previously lost in the mass of information sources. The presentation of humanists' scholarly results in electronic form is moving even faster. Precisely because of the complexities of the relationships they need to present, electronic "hypertext" books and journals are emerging. Indeed, they are emerging faster, with more vigor, and with more effect on their disciplines than are their counterparts in the sciences.

We all expect scientists and engineers to use computers in their research, but the notion that information technology could be central to humanistic scholarship is a bit more startling, at least to me. In large measure, it was talking about the application of computers to historiography and the theory of text that opened my eyes to the larger issues that I am trying to raise here. . . .

COMPUTERS AND TEACHING

The notion of computer-aided instruction has been touted for 30 years. Frankly, it has had relatively little impact, especially at the university level. The reason is obvious: Chalk and overhead projectors have been perfectly adequate technology given the current nature of scholarship and texts.

If, however, the professors are using information technology in their scholarship and the results of that scholarship can only be exhibited using the technology, the classroom will follow rapidly. How will it follow? Not, I think, by the "automated drill" scenario we have come to associate with computer-aided instruction.

These are interesting but mundane applications, mundane in the sense that they do not change the educational process in a deep way. More fundamental is the opportunity to involve students in the process of scholarship rather than merely its results. We like to say that we teach students to think, not merely to learn rote facts, but in truth we mostly limit them to thinking about what has been thought before. We can't ask them to explore new hypotheses because of the practicalities of access to sources and the sheer grunt work of collecting and analyzing data. Information technology eliminates those impediments.

A hint of this kind of change can be detected in a report in the *Chronicle of Higher Education* about the impact of the release of the *Thesaurus Linguae Graecae* on scholarship and education in the classics. The report noted that the release of this database, which includes virtually all Greek literature from Homer through the fall of Byzantium, has enabled undergraduate participation in research.

COMPUTERS AND INTERACTION WITH PROFESSORS

One cannot leave the subject of teaching without at least mentioning the issue of "productivity," the current code word to capture the public's frustration with the rising cost of college education and the perceived emphasis on research over teaching. The simplistic solution is to have professors spend more time in the classroom and less in the laboratory. Particularly given the wrenching restructuring that industry has undergone, the public has ample cause to ask why an elitist academe should be exempt from a reorientation toward greater customer satisfaction.

The irony, of course, is that one of the oldest figures of merit for any school—a low student/teacher ratio—is diametrically opposed to the strict definition of productivity as output per worker. Information technology is not going to resolve this tension; for our own children, we want relatively individual attention from the most qualified, intellectually alive professoriate possible. Information technology can, however, shift the focus of the discussion to the effectiveness and quality of the student/teacher interaction rather than just the number of contact hours.

Indeed, in modest ways it already has shifted that focus. By removing the barriers of space and time for example, e-mail has given my students much greater access to me than ever before. Involving students in the process of scholarship and giving them greater access to international authorities are more profound shifts, but I suspect that these are still just pale precursors of what we can do. Part and parcel of rethinking the impact of technology on the university is addressing precisely this issue.

THE UNIVERSITY AS PLACE

Technological change will even force us to reconsider some of the fundamental assumptions about what a university is. For example, historically a university has been a place. The stone walls of St. Benedict's cloister at Monte Cassino were the bastion that provided defense against the physical and intellectual vandals of the Dark Ages. In colonial times, Jefferson's Academical Village provided access to scholarly materials as well as collegial interaction by collocation. In contemporary times, scholars flock to scientific instruments and library collections. And, where the scholars assembled, the students followed.

In his influential 19th-century essays on the university, John Cardinal Newman wrote: "If I were asked to describe . . . what a university was, I should draw my answer from its ancient designation of a Stadium Generale. . . . This description implies the assemblage of strangers from all parts in one spot."

Newman then goes on at some length to emphasize that books are an inadequate source of true education and must be buttressed with discourse, which is obviously only feasible if the discussants are collocated. Thus the notion of being in one spot is, to him, essential to the very definition of the university; as he says, "else, how can there be any school at all?"

THE BENEFITS OF REMOTE SCHOLARSHIP

But with the possible exception of teaching, to which I'll return in a moment, I believe that information technology obviates the need for the university to be a place. With powerful ubiquitous computing and networking, I believe that each of the university's functions can be distributed in space, and possibly in time. Remote scholarship is the direct analog of telecommuting in the business world, and every bit as appealing. Academics tend to identify more closely with their disciplinary and intellectual colleagues than with their university. Freed from the need to be physically present in classroom, laboratory, or library, grouping by intellectual affinity may be more useful. But even then, physical grouping may be unnecessary.

There are some disciplines that need shared physical facilities, such as a telescope, that suggest the need of a place. But many large scientific instruments such as telescopes and accelerators are already run by consortia and shared by the faculty from many universities, and many of these facilities do not require the physical presence of the investigator, who could be on-line and have access through the network. Indeed, some instruments, such as those for space physics at Sondre Stomfjord in Greenland, are already accessed on the Internet. The university as place is already irrelevant to at least some scientific scholarship.

As with instruments in the sciences, direct access to archival materials is necessary for some humanistic scholarship but hardly all, and certainly not all of the time. If anything, the information infrastructure will provide greater access for a much larger set of scholars to archival materials of a quality that's "good enough." Consider the excitement caused by the recent release of the images of the Dead Sea Scrolls, even though the scrolls themselves are not accessible to most scholars.

As for teaching, we don't really know whether it can be distributed or not. I do know that even asking the question is considered heretical by some good teachers who contend that eyeball-to-eyeball contact is necessary. Others, including me, contend that although they need feedback to teach well, there is a threshold of fidelity beyond which one does not need to go; student and teacher probably don't need to smell one another, for example. Thus, there is some finite amount of information required to produce an adequate representation of the parties. If true, when that threshold of fidelity is reached electronically, high-quality teaching will be distributed. The fallacy in Newman's reasoning was only that he could not imagine quality discourse at a distance, but that is precisely what technology will enable.

UNCERTAINTIES

Can an institution such as the university, which has existed for a millennium and become an icon of our social fabric, disappear in a few decades because of technology? Of course. If you doubt it, check on the state of the family farm. Will the university as place in particular disappear? I expect not; the reduced importance of place does not imply no place. However, just as farming has been transformed, so will the university be. The everyday life of both faculty and students will be very different.

I have more questions than answers as to the shape of the new university. Having now laid the groundwork, let me pose a few of them:

• Will universities become mass-market manufacturers or distributors of information or will they be niche tutors to the privileged?

• Does it really make sense for every university to support the full complement of disciplines, or should they specialize and share courses in cyberspace? This might be a natural consequence of aggregation by disciplinary affinity.

• Might professors affiliate with several institutions or become freelance tutors to telepresent students? Indeed, might "tele-itinerant" scholars and tutors give new life to an ancient practice?

• Might some employers (and hence students) prefer a transcript that lists with whom certain courses have been taken rather than where?

• What about alumni and sports? Surely the allegiance of alumni to their alma mater has a great deal to do with place. Because the support of alumni is essential to universities, isn't that very human need sufficient to perpetuate university as place? Perhaps. But broad alumni support has become essential to the university only in relatively recent times. Moreover, alumni associations and large sports programs were created to support the university as place, not the other way around.

IS THE UNIVERSITY JUST A PLACE?

• Will universities merge into larger units as the corporate world has done or will the opposite happen? I can argue either side of this question. On the one hand, if a university isn't (just) a place, its major remaining function is certification: It certifies the competence of the faculty, programs, and graduates. We don't need thousands of organizations to do that. On the other hand, I can envision many small colleges being empowered to provide a broad curriculum through telelocation while retaining the intimacy so valued in our small liberal arts institutions. I don't know anyone that really wants the impersonal ambiance of a mega-university. The current size of these universities seems optimized for the physical infrastructure, not for either education or scholarship.

• Might the technology revive the talented amateur participation in the scientific community? Except in a few disciplines such as astronomy, the talented amateur has largely disappeared from scholarly discourse in science and engineering. Surely such individuals still exist, but they are isolated from the community of scholars. How can or should the university re-engage them?

• What about the various businesses such as the university press that have affiliated with universities? My guess is that each of these will be forced to rethink its principal mission and many will be irrelevant.

• Will more (most?) universities serve a global clientele, and how does that square with the publicly supported university in the United States? In particular, will private universities have greater flexibility to adapt to globalization, thus dooming the public universities?

• Does the function of socializing young adults, which perhaps remains a reason for "place," need to be coupled with the educational function or could it be done better by some form of social service?

Some will interpret these questions as threatening; I don't. That there will be a change seems inevitable. But change always implies opportunity; in this case, the opportunity to improve all facets of what we do in the academy. The challenge is to anticipate and exploit the changes.

"The [university] education of the
young is hardly possible in the
absence of close and intimate
educational interaction, mentoring,
and modeling."

THE INFORMATION REVOLUTION
WILL NOT OBVIATE THE UNIVERSITY

Majid Tehranian

Information technology is transforming and enhancing some of
the educational functions of traditional universities, admits Majid Tehranian in the following viewpoint. However, he argues,
computers and the Internet can never replace the moral education and socialization that the university experience provides to
students. Information technology can enhance learning, he asserts, but interaction between students and teachers at a university campus will always be an important aspect of education.
Tehranian is a professor of communications at the University of
Hawaii at Manoa.

As you read, consider the following questions:
1. According to Eli Noam, cited by Tehranian, what are the three
   primary functions of the university?
2. What are five other central functions of the university, in
   Tehranian's opinion?
3. How does the author define "transformative knowledge"?

Reprinted from "The End of the University?" by Majid Tehranian, *Information Society*,
October 1996, pp. 441–47, by permission of Taylor & Francis, Washington, D.C.

In an essay, Eli Noam has argued that the current telecommunication revolution is turning universities into dinosaurs. The three most important functions of the university (creation, preservation, and transmission of knowledge), he argues, are being rapidly usurped by the telecommunication networks (broadcasting, cable, Internet, World Wide Web).

Let us first look at the case for the end of university as we know it. Scientific knowledge, Noam argues, is growing exponentially at the rate of 4–8% per annum with a doubling period of 10–15 years. The main response to this phenomenal growth has been to specialize. But there are financial and physical limits to how specialized a university can get. The ever-narrowing experts, who get to know more and more about less and less, have had to find refuge elsewhere—in think tanks, consultancies, corporate research and development departments, and government research institutes. The first function of universities as creators of knowledge is thus being overtaken by the better funded and far more specialized government and private research institutions. Moreover, universities used to have the advantage of having a critical mass of scholars present on their campuses who could interact among themselves to the benefit of all, but modern transportation and telecommunication have offered alternatives that are rapidly growing in use.

TRADITIONAL FUNCTIONS OF THE UNIVERSITY

In fact, however, universities have never had a monopoly of knowledge in society. The modern electronic networks such as the print, broadcasting, and micromedia (copying machines, audio and video recorders, personal and laptop computers, etc.) have historically served to disperse and democratize knowledge. We should be all grateful for that. Cyberspace is further deschooling, or rather, schooling society. The real policy issue, however, is how to avoid a new kind of information feudalism that may come out of a total commercialization of the knowledge networks. If access to information becomes too costly and out of reach of the less fortunate in society, we may be facing a grim and explosive future in the development of a permanently unemployed and unemployable underclass. The recent rise of functional illiteracy in the United States to the alarming levels of about 28% is not a reassuring sign. Privatization of information in an information society is inevitably driving some information consumers out of the market. There is some historical precedent for this. In the English enclosure movement, common pasture land was gradually "enclosed" into private property for large-scale breeding of sheep and production of wool. Something like that is currently happening to public information, which is being rapidly processed into value-added networks (VANs) and priced out of the reach of common folks. For instance, Lexis-Nexis contains some 500 million documents growing at the rate of 30% per month. It is arguably the world's biggest electronic library, but access is limited to those few who can afford it. In a democratic society, the open access traditions of public universities and libraries must be maintained in order to avoid a bifurcation of society into information-rich and information-poor.

The second function of universities is the preservation of knowledge. Libraries as the repositories of such knowledge are often thought of as the heart of a university. But as the production of knowledge grows exponentially, so does the cost of acquisition and storage. "For example," Noam observes, "in 1940 an annual subscription to *Chemical Abstracts* cost $12; in 1977 it was $3500; and in 1995 it was $17,400." University libraries are thus finding it increasingly difficult to keep up with the volume and cost of information storage. Consequently, they are turning to investment in electronic access rather than physical storage. But universities have never had a monopoly in storage of knowledge, as witnessed by the public library system in the United States. Again, the challenge lies in making sure that the public and university libraries are enabled to catch up with the rapid rise in storage facilities by a shift to the new, cost- and space-saving technologies (on-line databases, optical disks, etc.).

The third function of universities is transmission of knowledge—their teaching role. "Already," Noam argues, "electronic distant education is available for a wide range of educational instruction through broadcast, cable, on-line, and satellite technologies." He goes on to cite the examples of Agricultural Satellite Network (AGSat), International University College, and Mind Extension University (on which Newt Gingrich has lectured), all of which employ communications technologies to offer courses of instruction entirely on their own or in cooperation with traditional institutions of higher education. To this we might add a number of others, including Arizona University with the largest on-line student registration in the United States and, increasingly, a number of on-line degree programs conducted by traditional universities.

THE DEMISE OF OTHER INSTITUTIONS

Are the cards thus stacked against conventional universities? Will they survive? Can they survive the combined blows of technological obsolescence, legislative underfunding, rising costs, moral browbeating, and declining numbers of students lured away to the new, perhaps more efficient, and less costly alternatives for higher education? A look at the origins of modern universities might provide a clue to what would probably happen. There is conclusive evidence to suggest that the invention of print technology in Europe undermined the authority of the Church and boosted the nascent secular institutions of learning in the modern universities at Padua, Bologna, Montpellier, Prague, Vienna, Paris, Oxford, Cambridge, and Heidelberg. However, the Church did not disappear from the face of the earth. It survived, but it was transformed from the monolithic institution that it used to be into a diversity of Catholic and Protestant churches reflecting national ethos, class divisions, and individual preferences. The rise of a new secular priesthood, namely, modern scientists, also gradually took away the monopoly that the Church enjoyed over revealed knowledge. The Bible became subject to a diversity of interpretations. Churches gradually became primarily the refuge for spiritual healing, social gathering, and moral education, rather than centers of learning.

COLLEGE AS COMMUNITY

True teaching and learning are about more than information and its transmission. Education is based on mentoring, internalization, identification, role modeling, guidance, socialization, interaction, and group activity. In these processes, physical proximity plays an important role. Thus, the strength of the future physical university lies less in pure information and more in college as a community; less in wholesale lecture, and more in individual tutorial; less in Cyber-U, and more in Goodbye-Mr.-Chips College. Technology would augment, not substitute, and provide new tools for strengthening community on campus, even beyond graduation.

Eli M. Noam, *Science*, October 13, 1995.

Similarly, the new network technologies are further dispersing the sources of production and distribution of knowledge. It is still hard to tell what impact they will have on conventional universities. However, it is safe to assume that universities have to respond to this challenge by reinventing themselves. Universities can no longer pretend to be the ivory towers of yesterday. Since the new network technologies are global in character, education must become global in scope. Since they have blurred the institutional boundaries between government, corporate, and academic worlds, universities must be willing to respond to the needs of other institutions in society. Since lifelong learning has become a necessity, they must also adapt their programs to suit an older generation of students. There is ample evidence to suggest that conventional universities are responding to all of these challenges. In fact, universities have been on the forefront of the educational uses of Internet and World Wide Web. We may criticize them for their institutional conservatism and slow rate of adaptation, but they are gradually adapting to a new open learning environment.

OTHER FUNCTIONS OF UNIVERSITIES

Noam neglects, however, to mention five other central functions of universities that cannot be easily performed by the networks. These may be considered to be *professional certification, moral education, scientific socialization, social criticism,* and *elite recruitment.* In modern societies, universities have served as the primary agents for the performance of these functions. Universities continue to be the main clearing house for educating and certifying the professionals in industrial societies. Other sectors of society have so far gladly relegated that function to universities, but if universities fail to keep up with the changing job markets, they will be replaced by other institutions. In the United States, there is already a corporate system of higher education that rivals conventional universities in its budgetary outlays. Moreover, conventional universities themselves are increasingly under the spell of corporate demands and patronage. In a *cri de coeur,* Lawrence C. Soley has lamented the corporate takeover of American universities during the past few decades. Governors of 11 Western states also met in Denver in 1995 to advance the cause of virtual universities in order to save on costs. In some states, demand for college education is expected to rise significantly, and the governors wish to preempt spiraling budgets. In Utah, for instance, it is projected to double in the next 20 years. The certification function of conventional universities can thus be passed on to virtual universities without much ado.

However, there are dissenting voices such as that of the governor of Hawaii, Benjamin Cayetano, who argues that many of his values were shaped during college and doubts if a virtual university can replace that. But universities' function of moral education has been under attack in recent decades. At a November 1995 Republican gathering, while introducing Rush Limbaugh, Newt Gingrich spoke of his genius and how it has been left uncorrupted because Limbaugh dropped out of college after his second semester! In the United States, under the banners of political correctness and its critics, the town–gown rituals of mutual recrimination have thus taken on new dimensions. Is a new Age of Darkness upon us? If conventional universities are disbanded tomorrow, society will have to reinvent them to provide for the moral education of the young during their most volatile, adolescent years. Otherwise, society may have to suffer the self-righteous arrogance of many half-educated and unreflective pundits and politicians. The moral moratorium of college campuses has worked in the past to refine the intellect and spirit of youth. In conjunction with other institutions in society such as the family, the church, and the schools, universities have an obligation to morally educate the young in our traditions of civility while allowing them to explore alternative life-styles and personal identities. In this process, too, cyberspace has already supplemented conventional campuses as the arena for migrating identities testing competing personas in their search for meaning, self-definition, and identity crisis resolution. Just like universities, the Internet also has come under attack by moralists for allowing "too much" self-expression.

DEVELOPING A LIFELONG HABIT OF LEARNING

Universities, most of all, teach students how to learn. Given the exponential growth rate of scientific knowledge, learning to learn is the best bequest students can receive from their education. This requires scientific socialization of a high order. The development of a scholarly temperament, including a passionate commitment to the search for truths combined with rigor and dispassion in method, tolerance in practice, and humility in errors, are all qualities that are often conspicuous by their absence on and off campuses. But those are the qualities that good universities nurture in their faculty and students. It is difficult to see how virtual universities by themselves can socialize the students in these values.

Closely related to this function, of course, is the universities' function of social criticism. Modern societies are, above all, reflexive societies. They monitor themselves and take note of errors of judgment and behavior in order to correct them. Universities, along with the religious and media institutions, are particularly charged with this responsibility. Modern universities are expected to criticize society from the standpoint of its own ethical standards. The principles of academic freedom and the tenure system have been established at the universities in order to safeguard their function of independent social criticism. During the past two decades, however, universities in the United States have been threatened by the excesses of censorship, self-censorship as well as vocationalization and commercialization of education. If critiques of conventional universities mean that they are not self-censoring, commercializing, and vocationalizing fast enough, that criticism is asking universities to change their fundamental character.

Finally, elite universities in the United States and elsewhere are also performing another function as well—elite recruitment. The high tuitions they require may be regarded not only as the going cost of education but also as the elite club membership fees. Former Harvard President Derek Bok once admonished that "if you think the price of education is too high, try ignorance." Rising tuitions, dwindling scholarship funds, increasing reliance upon corporate support, and the weakening of the middle classes are currently raising the moral and material price of elite education. A self-perpetuating and noncirculating elite threatens not only democracy but also the moral and political basis of its own legitimacy. Higher education faces a real threat of bifurcation into a system of conventional elite universities and an emerging system of virtual and ghetto universities tending to the needs of the masses.

The Importance of the University Setting

A liberal education, encompassing most of the foregoing functions, entails modeling, mentoring, nurturing, guidance, and interaction. It aims at the development of the whole character of a person rather than focusing only on the acquisition of certain facts or skills. This calls for the development of an inquisitive mind and a moral sense of rights and obligations toward the community at its progressively higher levels of order and complexity, from local to global. Physical proximity and interaction are the *sine qua non* of this kind of education. As distance becomes less and less important in acquiring *additive* knowledge (science and technology) through electronic networks, proximity will assume greater importance in obtaining *regenerative* (moral) and *transformative* (spiritual) knowledge. Regenerative knowledge is the kind of knowledge that each generation relearns through its own trials and errors, pains and sufferings. By contrast, transformative knowledge comes about only when and if the gap between additive knowledge and regenerative knowledge grows so wide that the need for a new paradigm of thinking is felt by all. Such may be the human conditions at the end of the twentieth century. We are passing from modernity to postmodernity. Linearity is dead, yet we hear "Long Live Linearity!" We are becoming aware of other ways of seeing, yet we insist on our own single-minded ways of perceiving. The world has become a single lifeboat in a vast and apparently lifeless universe. Yet our paradigms of thinking are still organized around single tribal, national, and institutional loyalties. In such a universe, once again, human intelligence has to adapt itself and its institutions to account for both distance and proximity, globality and locality, networks and institutions. The university of the future will be a combination of local nodes and global networks. It will hopefully combine the best features of face-to-face education and distance learning. In such a university, training can be relegated to the distant educational networks, but the education of the young is hardly possible in the absence of close and intimate educational interaction, mentoring, and modeling. Virtual universities will, no doubt, appear and expand. They may serve the purposes of new types of certification for mid-career professionals or those who have missed the opportunities of conventional universities. But if the experience of some of the most well-known distant learning systems, such as the British Open University, are any indication, those will succeed in such universities that have already acquired the self-discipline of autonomous learning, such as teachers and professionals of various kinds. From now on, quality education will have to combine face-to-face with distant learning.

How Universities Can Adapt

What are the implications of all of this for higher educational leaders? First, do not despair. Despite state budget cuts, declining federal support, and parental grudges against high tuition, universities are here to stay. Second, just like churches some 500 years ago, universities have to adjust to a new social, cultural, and educational environment in which new communication technologies are blurring the boundaries between formal and informal education, schooling and lifelong learning, as well as primary, secondary, and tertiary socialization. Technological transformation is, however, presenting both risks of obsolescence and opportunities for institutional self-renewal that can maximize open learning and minimize classroom drudgery. If all goes well, the entire human society will become a university without walls and national boundaries.

Learning how to learn is becoming, more than ever before, the central function of all schooling. Universities must diversify, localize, globalize, and socialize. In all of these efforts, the rigid boundaries between the hallowed halls of academe and disciplinary boundaries will have to give way to cooperation with other institutions of society in the lifelong education of its youth and an aging population. The universities of tomorrow will be even more diversified than they are today. Some will primarily respond to the specific training needs of the corporations that sponsor them. Others will focus on educating broadly and liberally. The corporate sector will be hopefully wise enough to allow the universities to carry the burden of responsibility and cost of screening the liberally educated employment candidates for them because they know such candidates make better employees.

At the same time, universities must localize by responding to the social, economic, and educational needs of their own immediate environment. The traditions of land-grant universities are, in this respect, very relevant. However, universities can no longer stay aloof from the global society that has rapidly come into existence by the global markets, job opportunities, and language and cultural learning that all of this demands. Last but not least, universities can no longer afford the dubious luxury of staying within their ivory towers, aloof from the other social institutions and assuming a supercilious attitude toward the religious, military, economic, and political values and norms. Universities must engage the other institutions of society in a critical dialogue on societal goals and plans that transcends institutional boundaries by offering lifelong educational opportunities to mid-career religious leaders, military officers, corporate executives, and politicians in order as much to teach as to learn from them. For universities, mastering the emerging technologies of learning and power is as much a key to such strategies of survival and prosperity as any other single factor.

PERIODICAL BIBLIOGRAPHY

The following articles have been selected to supplement the diverse views presented in this chapter. Addresses are provided for periodicals not indexed in the *Readers' Guide to Periodical Literature*, the *Alternative Press Index*, the *Social Sciences Index*, or the *Index to Legal Periodicals and Books*.

Nicholas C. Burbules	"Technology: What We Haven't Worried About," *Education Digest*, May 1997.
Paul Gruchow	"Ransacking Our Libraries," *Utne Reader*, May/June 1995.
Lisa Gubernick and Ashlea Ebeling	"I Got My Degree Through E-mail," *Forbes*, June 16, 1997.
Marilyn Gell Mason	"The Yin and Yang of Knowing," *Daedalus*, Fall 1996.
Richard L. Measelle	"Reinventing Education," *Vital Speeches of the Day*, June 1, 1996.
Kathryn C. Montgomery	"Children in the Digital Age," *American Prospect*, July/August 1996.
Eli M. Noam	"Electronics and the Dim Future of the University," *Science*, October 13, 1995.
Joseph N. Pelton	"Cyberlearning vs. the University," *Futurist*, November/December 1996.
Neil Postman	"Virtual Students, Digital Classroom," *Nation*, October 9, 1995.
Laura Shapiro	"What About Books?" *Newsweek*, July 7, 1997.
Nathaniel Sheppard Jr.	"Another Lane on the Superhighway," *Emerge*, July/August 1997. Available from 2425 W. Olympic Blvd., Suite 4050W, Santa Monica, CA 90404.
David Skinner	"Computers: Good for Education?" *Public Interest*, Summer 1997.
James H. Snider	"Education Wars: The Battle over Information-Age Technology," *Futurist*, May/June 1996.

Paul Starr   "Computing Our Way to Educational
                         Reform," *American Prospect*, July/August 1996.

Sallie Tisdale   "Silence, Please: The Public Library as
                         Entertainment Center," *Harper's*, March 1997.

Sherry Turkle   "Seeing Through Computers," *American Prospect*,
                         March/April 1997.

Velma A. Walker   "The Great Technology Divide: How Urban
                         Schools Lose," *Education Digest*, February 1997.

CHAPTER 3

WILL THE INFORMATION REVOLUTION TRANSFORM WORK?

CHAPTER PREFACE

In November 1994, twelve hundred employees of Bell-Atlantic, a Pennsylvania telecommunications company, went to work wearing T-shirts with graphic illustrations of themselves as "Information Highway Roadkill." The workers were protesting the announcement of fifty-six hundred layoffs, the latest in a series of Bell-Atlantic cutbacks that served as just one example of the massive elimination of jobs occurring throughout the telecommunications industry. These layoffs were the result of an increasing amount of industry contracts with cheaper labor overseas and the replacement of workers with machines and computers. According to York University history professor David Noble, "The very workers who are constructing the new information infrastructure are among the first to go, but not the only ones. The same fate is facing countless workers in manufacturing and service industries in the wake of the introduction of these new information technologies." Assembly-line workers, secretaries, bank tellers, telephone operators, librarians, sales clerks, and middle managers are examples of the kinds of workers whose jobs are destined for near extinction, analysts report.

Faced with this trend, many commentators have suggested various approaches to adjusting to life in an information-age economy. After four layoffs, former librarian Peggy Argus started working independently as a children's book distributor, freelance writer, and personal coach. Now making $37,000 a year working out of her home, Argus's goal is to "never have a 9-to-5 job again." She contends that information-age workers must arm themselves with technical skills and fortitude and prepare to take on multiple careers over the course of a lifetime. Economist Jeremy Rifkin, however, argues that individual workers should not be expected to bear the brunt of major economic changes. Corporations and governments must acknowledge the needs of the workforce during the transition to an information-age economy, he maintains. Rifkin proposes reducing the work week to thirty hours, which would enable new high-tech plants to employ more workers. If employees worked in shifts, companies could greatly boost productivity by operating on a twenty-four-hour basis, "and thus pay workers more for working less," Rifkin asserts.

The following chapter includes further discussion on the information revolution's transformation of the world of work.

> "In the years ahead, the workplace will become dramatically different . . . due to such factors as electronically linked work sites, [and] computerized coaching and monitoring equipment."

THE INFORMATION REVOLUTION WILL TRANSFORM THE WORKPLACE

Robert Barner

In the following viewpoint, Robert Barner predicts that workplaces of the future will become "virtual organizations," utilizing electronic links to connect far-flung workers and employing computerized monitoring systems to manage them. Companies will need to adapt their management techniques to meet the challenges presented by the information-age workplace, he argues. Barner is the vice president of Parry Consulting Services, Inc., a management consulting firm in Tequesta, Florida. He is also the author of *Crossing the Minefield: Tactics for Overcoming Today's Toughest Management Challenges.*

As you read, consider the following questions:

1. According to Barner, what three factors will fuel the growth of the virtual organization?
2. In the author's opinion, how can just-in-time workers be motivated in their work?
3. What is the biggest drawback to the use of electronic monitoring systems by companies, according to the author?

Reprinted from "Seven Changes That Will Challenge Managers—and Workers," by Robert Barner, Futurist, March/April 1996, by permission of the World Future Society, 7910 Woodmont Ave., Suite 450, Bethesda, MD 20814; (301) 656-8274; fax: (301) 951-0394; http://www.wfs.org/wfs.

In the years ahead, the workplace will become dramatically different from what it is now, due to such factors as electronically linked work sites, computerized coaching and monitoring equipment, and a more diverse work force.

To obtain firsthand information on the changes occurring in the workplace, during 1995 I conducted a detailed literary research of workplace trends, supplemented by five focus-group sessions and individual interviews involving over 200 work professionals, representing such diverse industries as telecommunications, electric utilities, retail sales, and governmental organizations.

What emerged from this research are the following trends that I believe will reshape work environments over the next 10 years.

THE VIRTUAL ORGANIZATION

We are rapidly moving toward a distributed work force that uses electronic technology to link workers and functions at scattered sites. This change is rapidly altering the nature of work, from the sales representative whose company database allows her to give customers immediate information on new product features, to the shipping employee who can monitor goods in real time.

The growth of the virtual organization will be fueled by three factors:

• The rapid evolution of electronic technologies, which are facilitating the digital, wireless transfer of video, audio, and text information.

• The rapid spread of computer networks, in which the United States now maintains a strong global advantage over many other countries, including Japan.

• The growth of telecommuting, which will enable companies to provide faster response to customers, reduce facility expenses, and help workers meet their child- and elder-care responsibilities.

One implication of this trend is that people will need to develop specialized communication and planning skills to succeed in the virtual-work environment. Traditionally, managers who lacked communication and planning skills often compensated for these skills through iterative face-to-face discussions, requiring team members to come back to them again and again to clarify performance goals or decision-making authority. To capitalize on the flexibility and speed that are possible through distributed, networked teams, managers and team members will have to form clear, upfront agreements regarding: (a) performance expectations; (b) the team's priorities; (c) how communications are to be carried out among members; and (d) the degree of resource support for telecommuters (e.g., dedicated business lines installed in the home or home-based printers).

Another challenge will be information overload—the kind that occurs when a worker finds 60 e-mail messages waiting. Some people are already finding ways to counter this through the use of "bozo filters"—software programs that automatically screen out the messages of certain e-mail senders.

To prevent information overload, communication skills will need to be geared for the virtual organization. An example is the ability to communicate electronically without the subtle, nonverbal cues that we get in face-to-face communications. When these cues are suddenly absent, as they are in e-mail correspondence, the result can be a misunderstanding or misinterpretation of messages that seem extremely blunt or antagonistic.

NETWORKS CHANGE DECISION-MAKING PROCESSES

Electronic networking can redistribute power in organizations. Computer networks make it technically feasible for employees to skip levels in the chain of command, providing senior managers with direct feedback on performance problems and questions regarding organizational issues. Electronic bulletin boards let workers anonymously raise organizational issues, and they provide an effective rumor-control mechanism. But networks can also make employees at remote sites feel as if they are part of the team.

Computer networks require faster decisions from both individuals and groups. Only a few years ago, many people relied on "float"—the gap between when you wrote a check and when the bank actually cashed it—as a safety buffer for ensuring sufficient funds. Computer technology has eliminated that financial float, and it has also eliminated decision float. Workers who are given immediate access to business information and feedback on team performance are under greater pressure to respond faster to organizational demands; those who demonstrate skills in fast-response decision making will find themselves in a strong, competitive position in the networked marketplace.

The virtual organization will also reshape traditional approaches to group decision making. Research done by Lee Sproull and Sara Kiesler, authors of Connections: New Ways of Working in the Networked Organization, suggests that, in contrast to face-to-face discussions, e-mail discussions make low-status individuals less hesitant to participate in discussions and to relinquish their points of view. As a result, e-mail decision-making sessions can take much longer to resolve—a phenomenon that runs counter to current pressures to streamline group decision making. This finding will have serious implications for organizations attempting to support employee empowerment and strengthen team performance.

To meet these challenges, workers will need to develop skills in network-based decision making, including the use of such specialized tools as group-decision-support software. Such tools will help to streamline decision making by enabling each worker to evaluate options without discussing it with the group, then automatically computing the team's overall decision. This approach offers obvious advantages for teams that are trying to coordinate efforts across different time zones or work shifts.

The virtual organization will change recruiting and career development. More headhunting firms and employees are using the Internet to match jobs and candidates. Organizations are using internal databases to profile employees' skills and find the most-qualified job candidates within the organization.

These changes will help employees identify alternative career targets and let cross-functional teams obtain the best possible mix of technical skills. Employee-skill databases will also make it more difficult for managers to hoard talent within their own teams.

THE JUST-IN-TIME WORK FORCE

In the United States, the number of individuals employed by temporary agencies has increased 240% in the last 10 years. Along with using more just-in-time workers, organizations are also streamlining operations and reducing costs by outsourcing support functions such as information services, security, and human resources.

Finding new ways to motivate temporary employees will become a key issue. When organizations fail to address this issue, problems can occur in performance and morale. A recent Fortune article cites Kolmar Laboratories, a New York–based cosmetics firm, which experienced conflicts when the full-time employees tried to pressure temporary workers (almost half of the company's assembly work force) to speed up their production. Full-time workers were already motivated to increase their productivity, since they were being paid according to their production levels. But the temporary workers earned a flat hourly rate and therefore had no incentive to work harder or faster.

This example illustrates the difficulty of motivating just-in-time workers, who lack traditional motivators such as promotions, merit increases, and profit-sharing programs. Just-in-time workers will be encouraged to take a higher degree of ownership in their work by providing them with access to information and training—formerly the prerogative of full-time staff. Another morale-boosting motivator is to solicit input and ideas from just-in-time workers.

In tomorrow's workplace, new just-in-time workers will need to be brought up to speed more quickly on company policies, procedures, and work practices. The issue of new-employee orientation is particularly important for highly paid professional positions such as engineers, computer programmers, and human resources personnel—areas experiencing rapid growth in just-in-time employees. Companies simply won't be able to afford to let such individuals gradually become acquainted with the workings of the organization. Electronic performance-support systems are one way to help increase the effectiveness of company orientation programs, providing just-in-time workers with real-time coaching and automated decision making.

THE ASCENDANCY OF KNOWLEDGE WORKERS

We are rapidly shifting from a work force that produces products to one that primarily manages information. Perhaps the fastest-growing segment of the knowledge work force is composed of technical specialists, such as medical technologists, paralegals, and computer installers, who have proliferated as a direct result of the growing need for hands-on technical experts who can support new technologies. Another factor has been the need for employers in fields such as law and medicine to reduce labor costs by shifting responsibilities to technical assistants.

The rapid growth of knowledge workers will require organizations to rethink their traditional approaches to directing, coaching, and motivating employees. In addition, as companies continue to downsize, they will be less willing to pay for "managerial purists"—people who do nothing but manage. Instead, managers will be expected to contribute technical expertise to their jobs and to be willing to roll up their sleeves and contribute when necessary.

Given the shrinking half-life for many technical skills, this change will place managers under additional pressure to avoid technical obsolescence. As an example, consider how long current software or engineering managers can afford to lag behind new technical developments before finding themselves hopelessly outdated. Managers will have to make a strong commitment to lifelong learning and skill advancement to achieve job security in the new work environment.

Given an increasingly mobile work force, tomorrow's managers will need to provide their teams with the historical context needed to understand the workings of the organization.

As corporate downsizings force knowledge workers to market themselves to a variety of companies, managers will have to continually educate new employees on corporate culture and values.

COMPUTERS AND THE INTERNATIONAL ECONOMY

Human power is becoming increasingly ineffective in controlling the way information technology shapes our economic and political lives. Geographic location of resources, labor, and capital means less as scattered countries use information technologies to work together. Many cars have parts made in a half dozen countries; stores sell look-alike clothes sewn on four continents. The reason? Management can control quality and coordinate production without regard to place or distance. Money moves most easily. Stocks, currency, and bonds traded on worldwide electronic markets amount to an estimated three trillion dollars each day, twice the annual U.S. budget.

Joel L. Swerdlow, *National Geographic*, October 1995.

Knowledge about what was accomplished with the company's clients two years ago may get lost when the staff reshuffles, so managers will have to become repositories for organizational history. Some companies are beginning to respond to this challenge by factoring in human knowledge as a key component of their asset base and by creating cross-indexed "knowledge bases" that enable workers to shorten learning curves by tapping into each others' experiences.

Organizations will also be challenged to build effective team relationships between two different levels of knowledge workers—professionals and paraprofessionals. There is a growing potential for conflict between broad-based professionals and lower-paid technical specialists who are extremely skilled within a relatively narrow spectrum of their career field.

COMPUTERIZED COACHING AND ELECTRONIC MONITORING

Over the next 10 years, there will be a dramatic increase in the use of electronic systems to accelerate employee learning, augment decision making, and monitor performance. Proponents of these systems argue that they enable employees to learn their jobs faster, provide workers and managers with immediate performance feedback, and make it easier to pinpoint performance problems in large call-in centers.

The biggest drawback of electronic monitoring systems is that they can make employees feel helpless, manipulated, and exploited. Some employees might feel that their managers are using these tools to peer over their shoulders electronically. This could put many management-employee relationships under great stress. To address these concerns, organizations will need to ensure that managers use electronic monitoring systems appropriately in order to avoid legal challenges of misuse.

As we move toward the virtual organization over the next few years, it will become more difficult to delineate the dividing line between work and home, and to determine when an employee's rights of privacy have been violated. For example, should an e-mail message sent to an employee's home at 9 p.m. be viewed as an inherent feature of the networked job, or does it constitute a personal infringement on an employee's privacy?

Electronic "performance enhancement" systems will also decrease employees' dependence on managers for coaching, training, and performance feedback and help make self-directed learning a reality. While this will free up the manager's time, some managers may feel that these changes will threaten their traditional roles as coaches and advisers.

THE GROWTH OF WORKER DIVERSITY

In the next 10 years, worker diversity will become a critical issue. One reason is that, by the year 2000, 85% of people entering the U.S. job market for the first time will be women and minorities, and just 15% will be white males, according to U.S. Labor Department projections. Another factor is that companies are increasingly setting up manufacturing and assembly plants in other countries, and many smaller companies are expanding into international markets.

As a result, during the next few years many people will have their first experiences with multicultural work groups and will need to adapt to different work expectations and communication styles. Added to these changes is the explosion of computer networks. When we consider the phenomenon of flaming, it becomes easy to understand the types of e-mail based, cross-cultural communication breakdowns that could be generated as a byproduct of increased global interconnectivity.

These factors will encourage organizations to value highly

those workers and managers who can operate within diversified employee groups. Sensitivity training will help managers understand the needs and perspectives of different members in work groups, including white male employees who may feel disenfranchised from their former power base. Companies will also need to become more adept at assessing workers' potential for success within long-term, multicultural, high-risk work assignments. . . .

THE BIRTH OF THE DYNAMIC WORK FORCE

Work methods and functions are no longer permanent and immutable structures; they are fluid processes that require workers to adapt continuously. Organizations will be forced to question many of the "stable state" assumptions under which they've traditionally operated, such as who their competitors are and who their potential customers may be. For example, U.S. defense contractors are now shifting from governmental to commercial markets, while companies such as Motorola and Federal Express are recognizing the strong market advantage that can be obtained by meeting the growing customer demand for fast response in product design and delivery.

One impact of these trends is that, over the next few years, managerial performance will be based less on the ability to direct and coordinate work functions and more on improving key work processes.

Within stable-state organizations, a good manager is viewed as someone who consistently maintains solid performance within a team, while company loyalty is synonymous with defending the value of the organization's policies, procedures, and processes. In contrast, the dynamic organization recognizes the need for continuous improvement to meet changing customer requirements and competitor actions. In such organizations, managers will be increasingly judged on their ability to identify and implement improvements and to encourage innovative thinking from team members, while professionals will be judged on their ability to adapt quickly to widely different work environments.

Finally, the dynamic organization will require workers to be able to jump quickly into new ventures and manage temporary, project-focused teams, as more and more of their work responsibilities will lie outside of the traditional "work niche" consisting of a rigid job description and functional organizational "home."

"[New technologies] are often designed and developed with a disdain for the workforce."

THE TRANSFORMATION OF THE WORKPLACE WILL BE NEGATIVE

Charley Richardson

The introduction of technological innovations in the workplace, which are designed to increase productivity, often causes job loss and injury or overstressing of workers, Charley Richardson contends in the following viewpoint. Technology's biggest impact, however, is its damaging effect on the relationship between workers and managers, he argues. Management uses new technology to replace employee skills and knowledge, Richardson maintains, leaving the workforce without its traditional source of power for bargaining with management. Richardson is the director of the Technology and Work Program at the University of Massachusetts in Lowell.

As you read, consider the following questions:

1. According to Richardson, what is the true significance of technology?
2. In the author's opinion, what is the core point about technology's social impact and effect on jobs?
3. What is the source of power for management, according to the author?

Reprinted from "Computers Don't Kill Jobs, People Do: Technology and Power in the Workplace," by Charley Richardson, *Annals of the American Academy of Political and Social Science*, vol. 544, March 1996, by permission of Sage Publications, Inc., copyright ©1996 by The American Academy of Political and Social Science.

The American workplace is undergoing massive change. *BusinessWeek* speaks of a "revolution in America's workplace," invoking the law of the jungle and warning that only some will prosper, only the strong will survive: "It's getting positively Darwinian. The American workplace, once a protected habitat offering a measure of prosperity in exchange for a lifetime of dedicated work, is now a dangerous place."

In calling up the ghost of Darwin (and social Darwinism), *Business Week* manages to avoid, for itself and for its readership, any responsibility for the outcomes of the "revolution": "There are no villains at work, just the inexorable forces of economic and technological change. The remaking of the world of work is but a means to one end—boosting productivity."

Even *Business Week*, though, has to admit that the changes in the workplace are hurting people: "If there are no villains, there are certainly victims. . . . These are difficult times for many working people in America."

TECHNOLOGY TRANSFERS POWER

Many others have detailed the disaster that is becoming the daily experience of working Americans. In this viewpoint, I examine one central aspect of the changes that are occurring in the workplace: new technology. I argue that, rather than an "inexorable force," technology is a critical, socially defined component of the move to reorganize America's workplaces. This reorganization has among its goals achieving massive increases in productivity, quality, and market sensitivity and flexibility, but it also seeks to vastly increase the power of management in relation to the workforce. Understanding the transfer of power that technology enables is critical to understanding and improving the future prospects for American workers.

Descriptions of technology as an independent and uncontrollable force—defined as progress—reflect the author's comfort with the social impact of technology or, at a minimum, with the general nature of the transfer of resources and power. Meanwhile, those who write with concern about the impacts of technological change but ignore the role of technology in transferring power risk directing attention away from the critical issue and providing an inappropriate foundation for policy prescriptions.

New workplace technologies are being introduced at an ever increasing rate. At the same time, the scope (breadth of impact) and penetration (depth of impact) of technological change are growing rapidly. In the course of this change, the boundaries of skill and geography that placed limits on management and provided leverage to the workforce are being broken by the move toward workerless factories, expert systems, and distributed activities linked by an information superhighway. Social regulation and labor-management interaction designed for a static and geographically constrained workplace are proving ineffective in protecting workers in the workplace of the future.

NEW TECHNOLOGY AND THE WORKER

While our social fascination with technology often focuses on what it can do in technical terms—how many millions of instructions per second, for example—or what an individual could do with it, technology's true significance lies in the choices that it provides within society and to whom it provides them. A laptop computer and global positioning system used in the woods to guide a hiker and keep a journal have primarily an individual significance. The same pieces of technology when placed in a tractor trailer and used to continuously monitor a driver's activities, without the consent of the driver, are highly socially significant and represent a loss of power or control by the driver.

The discussion of the technical aspects of technological change and the analysis of the changing workplace and its negative impacts on the workforce remain disconnected and insignificant without the link of social power. Like technojunkies, people are forced not only to take the new technologies that are offered to them but also to like them enough to call them progress and to call for more. They become convinced that the increases in productivity and quality that the dealers of technology promise will somehow solve the poverty, pollution, displacement, and disempowerment that accompanied the last round of technological change.

The real question that must be answered is being ignored or missed. Before asking what we are going to do about the loss of jobs due to technology and the poverty that accompanies it, we need to be asking, Why does a massive increase in the productive capacity of people lead to a decrease in the quality of life for the vast majority? Only by answering that question can we take aim at the cause rather than the symptoms.

New technology does not kill jobs; people do. Technology provides the means and allows job loss to be named progress. But people decide what kinds of technology to develop and how and when to use it. It is to the social dimensions of technological change and, in particular, to its impact on power relations in society that we must ultimately turn our attention.

The impacts of technological change in the workplace are a

product of the social process of design, development, and implementation. New workplace technologies emerge from a system that is generally unresponsive to the needs of the broad populace and over which the broad populace exerts little or no control. This system is staffed by people who speak in a different language from that of most people, who live in different communities, who work in different worlds, and who, in many ways, are taught to ignore, demean, and eliminate the workforce.

A DARK VIEW OF NEW TECHNOLOGY

Most progressives . . . take a [dark] view of the new technology, emphasizing its capitalist character and its tendency to extend and deepen the harsh consequences of capitalist relations of production. They point to the use of computerized technology and networks to extend employer control over workers, even over long distances, and to create automatic systems that can replace the judgement and discretion of expert employees. The re-emergence of home work in the age of the computer represents to these critics, not the advent of decentered, autonomous work but the growth of contingent, insecure employment, the cheapening of production, and the intensification of work. It also reproduces and reinforces traditional patterns of gender subordination under capitalism, as women workers are obliged to take low-wage, insecure jobs that simultaneously perpetuate their status as the sole providers of (unpaid) child care and domestic labor.

Peter Meiksins, *Monthly Review*, July/August 1997.

While much of the research and development is controlled by the private sector (obviously out of reach of the public and the workforce), even public intervention and funding do little to improve the situation. The Advanced Technology Program (ATP) of the National Institute of Standards and Technology (NIST) has [since 1994] been holding meetings to discuss the technologies that need to be developed for the future, with the purpose of guiding government funding. The attendees at these sessions are a clear indication of who makes the decisions about technology.

One such meeting was directed at technology in health care. But who was in attendance? It was not nurses. It was not dietary aides. It was not nurse's aides. It was the big hospitals, but it was also McDonnell Douglas, IBM, and Digital Equipment Corporation—large corporations looking for new markets in which to push their technologies, large corporations that are known for their recent downsizing and lack of concern for the workforce.

Technologies are designed, developed, and implemented with little or no attention to the needs of the workforce or the impact that the technologies might have on the workforce. In fact, they are often designed and developed with a disdain for the workforce. Technologies are then used to increase control over and decrease reliance on the workforce, and it is from here that the impacts of technological change emerge.

GOING BEYOND THE LOSS OF JOBS

Much of the discussion about technology's social impact has focused on the effects on jobs and skills. The great debates over whether technology is a net destroyer or net creator of jobs and whether it increases or decreases skills have been endless. While interesting, these debates miss the core point; net impacts are not the issue. The real questions are not how many jobs and how much skill but who has them, what kinds of leverage they provide, and what they mean in a social context.

Surely people do seem to lose their jobs due to new technology. But more bluntly put, and more accurately described, they are no longer needed by those who have the power to decide. The process can be done without them, and so they no longer have any value.

Technology also changes the skills that are needed to complete the production or service delivery process. For those possessing the no-longer-needed skills, it matters little whether or not the net effect is "up-skilling." Who has access to the new skills? At what cost? Are the new skills connected to the power base of the workforce (the union), or are they held by people who have been legally and/or culturally tied to management? These are the questions that need to be explored.

THE NEGATIVE IMPACTS OF TECHNOLOGY

Even those who survive technological displacement do not avoid the negative impacts of technology on the workplace. New technologies have been used to create workplaces where people are continuously monitored, where processes are increasingly lean, where repetitive strain injuries (RSIs) are commonplace, where stress is increasing, where new chemical hazards are introduced daily, and where dull and dead-end occupations reign.

The negative impacts of technological change on the workforce are rarely accidents. There are certainly thousands of examples of technologies that were built and implemented without allowing for the operator. But even these can hardly be called accidents, for the decision to ignore and demean the workforce was taken consciously decades ago and is still built into the education of engineers and the systems of technology design and implementation.

The vast majority of problems connected with technological change are in fact the result of intentional design. The designs were intentional, the outcomes were desired, and the impacts on the workforce were either ignored or depersonalized to the point that they became irrelevant. No one particularly wanted to create joblessness in society, but some did want to eliminate certain jobs. No one particularly wanted to eliminate people's skills, but some did want to make them irrelevant to the production and service delivery process—which is essentially the same thing. No one wanted to cause stress-related illness, but some did want to monitor and measure, to increase demand and decrease control—all of which contribute directly to stress.

No one wanted to increase the incidence of RSIs, but some did want to intensify work, eliminate downtime, and, in the process, increase repetition—all of which help create RSIs.

THE EFFECTS OF WORK STATION DESIGN

We can look at RSIs and stress as examples. There are four basic risk factors for RSIs: force, awkward posture, repetition, and lack of rest or recovery time. Force and awkward posture are mistakes. They could be called accidents of design. Somebody forgot to think about the person who is actually doing the job. The current focus on the redesign of work stations according to ergonomic principles is aimed at fixing some of the force and awkward-posture issues.

Repetition and no rest are different matters, however. Repetition and no rest are, in fact, design goals of a technology design, of workplace design. Just-in-time (JIT) systems and lean production are aimed at eliminating rest and increasing repetition. It is perhaps ironic, and perhaps sinister, that even some of the so-called ergonomic improvements that are being made, while eliminating force and awkward posture, are increasing lack of rest and repetition and may therefore be having a net negative impact on RSIs.

The stress resulting from computer monitoring of the workforce is another example of an impact that is the direct result of conscious design. It is no accident that in most workplaces, some form of computer monitoring is occurring. Despite this, there have yet to be any real analyses of the impact of computer monitoring on the workforce. We do know that lack of control and increased demand, both of which can result from continuous monitoring, are key sources of stress and causes of stress-related illness.

Those who have never been monitored at work should think about what it is like to drive a car with a police officer behind you, even if you routinely obey the traffic laws. Computers are the officer that is always behind you when you are at work.

Technologies have a significant impact on the conditions under which people work. Of that there is no doubt. Further, it is clear that many of the negative impacts of workplace technology grow directly out of a technological system that tends to ignore the needs of the workforce. While it would seem that technology would provide the basis for improving conditions for the workforce, the opposite seems to be the case in most instances. It is to the question of power—of why the system can ignore the vast majority and how technology ultimately affects power relations—that we must now turn our attention.

TECHNOLOGY AS AN INSTRUMENT OF POWER

If the impacts of technology can be connected to a social process of design, then the questions of who controls the decision making and in whose interests decisions are being made rise to the top. While this analysis is relatively straightforward, we must now turn our attention to the ways in which decisions about technology affect power relations within the workplace. The main and most significant impact of technological change is not RSI, is not stress, and is not job loss. These are in fact merely symptoms of an overwhelming loss of power on the part of the vast majority.

If the workforce had the power to demand or take breaks or to slow the work down, RSIs and stress would be much less of a problem. If the workforce had the power to refuse weekend work or 12-hour shifts, their lives would be less harried and more controlled. If the workforce had the power to share productivity gains, wages would rise and the workweek could be shortened. If the workforce had the power to stop displacement, retraining for new technologies and new skills would become part of what employers do. If the workforce had the power to just say no to harmful technologies, the development process would change to reflect their needs and concerns.

On 3 July 1995, the New York Times published an article titled, "The New World of Work, Where Employers Call All the Shots." The article describes the declining ability of the workforce to have a say in the workplace, pointing to weaker unions, global competition, and new technology as the key ingredients leading to increasing insecurity for the workforce. It also notes that along with diminished job security, workers have experienced diminished bargaining power. They are losing the ability to negotiate, for example, for higher wages and improved health benefits.

Rather than being one of three factors, technology needs to be seen as a key to all the changes in power in the workplace. Certainly, the decline of unions has been supported by technological changes that have eliminated traditional skills, automated union jobs, and allowed work to be moved easily to nonunion plants, nonunion areas, and even other countries. Technology, in making it easier to move work around, has created much of the competition that we now complain about.

THE SOURCES OF POWER IN THE WORKPLACE

To understand the impact of technology on power in the workplace, we need to examine the sources of that power. For the workforce, power comes fundamentally from management's reliance on a certain set of workers to produce a product, provide a service, and, ultimately, make a profit. Management's power comes from the fact that it owns or controls the organization, the process, and the technology and from the fact that the workforce is dependent on the workplace to earn a living.

Technology can be seen as knowledge that is embedded in a production or service process, in a piece of equipment, in a material, or in a piece of software. Changes in technology therefore can affect whose knowledge and effort are necessary to production. Technology is often designed to capture knowledge and experience (or to make them irrelevant), and thus it changes the leverage of those with control over traditional skills. Expert systems, computer monitoring, statistical process control (SPC), and computer numerical controls (CNC) are examples of technologies that are designed specifically to capture and/or displace the knowledge of the workforce, thereby making the existing workforce less necessary.

Technology is also developed with the purpose of exerting control over effort and providing access to an increased effort pool (labor market). Computer monitoring and machine-paced processes are examples of technologies that help to control effort, while the information superhighway and electronic controls are designed and implemented specifically to enhance the transferability of work, thereby expanding the available effort pool to encompass the entire world population.

In these days of empowerment rhetoric, it is probably unfashionable to talk about disempowerment, but specific analysis of workplace technologies shows the workforce to be suffering from a massive erosion of bargaining power. Technology's "power to . . ." can generally be translated into "power over . . ." and the workforce is, first and foremost, on the short end.

AN IMBALANCE OF POWER

The mantra "workforce involvement," which dominates much of the management literature, implies synergy—that both parties gain more from the relationship than from the lack of a relationship. Workers are told that new technologies will benefit both parties and that therefore it is in the interest of the workforce to help implement technological changes.

Technology undoubtedly contributes to productivity, which should, of course, make more available to all. But buried (not too deeply) in the very innovations that increase the productive capacity of the workforce are factors that serve to deny the workforce the bargaining power to gain their share of the output. Realization of synergy assumes a balance of power between the workforce and management that does not exist now. In fact, the imbalance of power is increasing with technological change. Like a breeder reactor that makes its own fuel, technology, developed and implemented by and in the interest of those with power, in turn enhances that power and helps to undermine the countervailing power of other groups in society, particularly the workforce.

| "Sophisticated computers, robots, telecommunications, and other Information *Age* technologies are replacing human beings in nearly every [job] sector."

THE INFORMATION REVOLUTION WILL ELIMINATE JOBS

Jeremy Rifkin

In the following viewpoint, Jeremy Rifkin argues that information age technology will automate most traditional jobs and will fail to create enough new jobs to absorb the displaced workers. A new labor movement that focuses on achieving shorter workweeks and higher pay could help ameliorate the negative effects of the Information Age, he contends. Rifkin is president of the Foundation on Economic Trends in Washington, D.C., and the author of *The End of Work: The Decline of the Global Labor Force and the Dawn of the Post-Market Era*.

As you read, consider the following questions:

1. In Rifkin's estimate, how many jobs are potentially vulnerable to displacement by automation?
2. What are the two Achilles' heels of the Information Age, according to Rifkin?
3. In the author's opinion, what concerns of women workers could revitalize unions and the labor movement?

Reprinted from "Vanishing Jobs," by Jeremy Rifkin, *Mother Jones*, September/October 1995, by permission of *Mother Jones* magazine; ©1995, Foundation for National Progress.

"**W**ill there be a job for me in the new Information Age?" This is the question that most worries American voters—and the question that American politicians seem most determined to sidestep. President Bill Clinton warns workers that they will have to be retrained six or seven times during their work lives to match the dizzying speed of technological change. Speaker of the House Newt Gingrich talks about the "end of the traditional job" and advises every American worker to become his or her own independent contractor.

But does the president really think 124 million Americans can reinvent themselves every five years to keep up with a high-tech marketplace? Does Gingrich honestly believe every American can become a freelance entrepreneur, continually hustling contracts for short-term work assignments?

Buffeted by these unrealistic employment expectations, American workers are increasingly sullen and pessimistic. Most Americans have yet to recover from the recovery of 1993–1995, which was essentially a "jobless" recovery. While corporate profits are heading through the roof, average families struggle to keep a roof over their heads. More than one-fifth of the workforce is trapped in temporary assignments or works only part time. Millions of others have slipped quietly out of the economy and into an underclass no longer counted in the permanent employment figures. A staggering 15 percent of the population now lives below the official poverty line.

HIGH-TECH OPTIMISM VS. WORKERS' PESSIMISM

Both Clinton and Gingrich have asked American workers to remain patient. They explain that declining incomes represent only short-term adjustments. Democrats and Republicans alike beseech the faithful to place their trust in the high-tech future—to journey with them into cyberspace and become pioneers on the new electronic frontier. Their enthusiasm for technological marvels has an almost camp ring to it. If you didn't know better, you might suspect Mickey and Pluto were taking you on a guided tour through the Epcot Center.

Jittery and genuinely confused over the yawning gap between the official optimism of the politicians and their own personal plight, middle- and working-class American families seem to be holding on to a tiny thread of hope that the vast productivity gains of the high-tech revolution will somehow "trickle down" to them in the form of better jobs, wages, and benefits. That thread is likely to break by election time [November 1996] if, as I anticipate, the economy skids right by the soft landing predicted by the Federal Reserve Board and crashes headlong into a deep recession.

The Labor Department reported that payrolls sank by 101,000 workers in May 1995 alone—the largest drop in payrolls since April 1991, when the U.S. economy was deep in a recession. In June 1995, overall unemployment remained virtually unchanged, but manufacturing jobs declined by an additional 40,000. At the same time, inventories are up and consumer spending and confidence are down—sure signs of bad economic times ahead.

The psychological impact of a serious downturn coming so quickly upon the heels of the last one would be devastating. It is likely to set the framework for a politically wild roller-coaster ride for the rest of the 1990s, opening the door not only to new parties but to extralegal forms of politics.

THE INFORMATION REVOLUTION IS ELIMINATING JOBS

Meanwhile, few politicians and economists are paying attention to the underlying causes of—dare we say it?—the new "malaise" gripping the country. Throughout the current [1995] welfare reform debate, for example, members of both parties have trotted onto the House and Senate floors to urge an end to welfare and demand that all able-bodied men and women find jobs. Maverick Sen. Paul Simon (D-Ill.) has been virtually alone in raising the troubling question: "What jobs?"

The hard reality is that the global economy is in the midst of a transformation as significant as the Industrial Revolution. We are in the early stages of a shift from "mass labor" to highly skilled "elite labor," accompanied by increasing automation in the production of goods and the delivery of services. Sophisticated computers, robots, telecommunications, and other Information Age technologies are replacing human beings in nearly every sector. Factory workers, secretaries, receptionists, clerical workers, salesclerks, bank tellers, telephone operators, librarians, wholesalers, and middle managers are just a few of the many occupations destined for virtual extinction. In the United States alone, as many as 90 million jobs in a labor force of 124 million are potentially vulnerable to displacement by automation.

A few mainstream economists pin their hopes on increasing job opportunities in the knowledge sector. Secretary of Labor Robert Reich, for example, talks incessantly of the need for more highly skilled technicians, computer programmers, engineers, and professional workers. He barnstorms the country urging workers to retrain, retool, and reinvent themselves in time to gain a coveted place on the high-tech express.

The secretary ought to know better. Even if the entire workforce could be retrained for very skilled, high-tech jobs—which, of course, it can't—there will never be enough positions in the elite knowledge sector to absorb the millions let go as automation penetrates into every aspect of the production process.

It's not as if this is a revelation. For years the Alvin Tofflers and the John Naisbitts of the world have lectured the rest of us that the end of the industrial age also means the end of "mass production" and "mass labor." What they never mention is what "the masses" should do after they become redundant.

WILL THERE BE NEW JOBS IN THE FUTURE?

Laura D'Andrea Tyson, who now heads the National Economic Council, argues that the Information Age will bring a plethora of new technologies and products that we can't as yet even anticipate, and therefore it will create many new kinds of jobs. After a debate with me on CNN, Tyson noted that when the automobile replaced the horse and buggy, some people lost their jobs in the buggy trade but many more found work on the assembly line. Tyson believes that the same operating rules will govern the information era.

Tyson's argument is compelling. Still, I can't help but think that she may be wrong. Even if thousands of new products come along, they are likely to be manufactured in near-workerless factories and marketed by near-virtual companies requiring ever-smaller, more highly skilled workforces.

This steady decline of mass labor threatens to undermine the very foundations of the modern American state. For nearly 200 years, the heart of the social contract and the measure of individual human worth have centered on the value of each person's labor. How does society even begin to adjust to a new era in which labor is devalued or even rendered worthless?

LESSONS FROM PAST WORKER DISPLACEMENTS

This is not the first time the issue of devalued human labor has arisen in the history of the United States. The first group of Americans to be marginalized by the automation revolution was black men, more than 40 years ago. Their story is a bellwether.

In the mid-1950s, automation began to take a toll on the nation's factories. Hardest hit were unskilled jobs in the industries where black workers concentrated. Between 1953 and 1962, 1.6 million blue-collar manufacturing jobs were lost. In an essay, "Problems of the Negro Movement," published in 1964, civil rights activist Tom Kahn quipped, "It's as if racism, having put the Negro in his economic place, stepped aside to watch technology destroy that 'place.'"

Millions of African-American workers and their families became part of a perpetually unemployed "underclass" whose unskilled labor was no longer required in the mainstream economy. Vanquished and forgotten, many urban blacks vented their frustration and anger by taking to the streets. The rioting began in Watts in 1965 and spread east to Detroit and other Northern industrial cities.

Today, the same technological and economic forces are beginning to affect large numbers of white male workers. Many of the disaffected white men who make up ultraright-wing organizations are high school or community college graduates with limited skills who are forced to compete for a diminishing number of agricultural, manufacturing, and service jobs. While they blame affirmative action programs, immigrant groups, and illegal aliens for their woes, these men miss the real cause of their plight—technological innovations that devalue their labor. Like African-American men in the 1960s, the new militants view the government and law enforcement agencies as the enemy. They see a grand conspiracy to deny them their basic freedoms and constitutional rights. And they are arming themselves for a revolution.

ECONOMIC PROBLEMS RESULTING FROM THE LOSS OF JOBS

The Information Age may present difficulties for the captains of industry as well. By replacing more and more workers with machines, employers will eventually come up against the two economic Achilles' heels of the Information Age. The first is a simple problem of supply and demand: If mass numbers of people are underemployed or unemployed, who's going to buy the flood of products and services being churned out?

The second Achilles' heel for business—and one never talked about—is the effect on capital accumulation when vast numbers of employees are let go or hired on a temporary basis so that employers can avoid paying out benefits—especially pension fund benefits. As it turns out, pension funds, now worth more than $5 trillion in the United States alone, keep much of the capitalist system afloat. For nearly 25 years, the pension funds of millions of workers have served as a forced savings pool that has financed capital investments.

Pension funds account for 74 percent of net individual savings, more than one-third of all corporate equities, and nearly 40 percent of all corporate bonds. Pension assets exceed the assets of commercial banks and make up nearly one-third of the total financial assets of the U.S. economy. In 1993 alone, pension funds made new investments of between $1 trillion and $1.5 trillion.

If too many workers are let go or marginalized into jobs without pension benefits, the capitalist system is likely to collapse slowly in on itself as employers drain it of the workers' funds necessary for new capital investments. In the final analysis, sharing the vast productivity gains of the Information Age is absolutely essential to guarantee the well-being of management, stockholders, labor, and the economy as a whole.

Toles. ©1995 Universal Press Syndicate. Reprinted with permission.

Sadly, while our politicians gush over the great technological breakthroughs that lie ahead in cyberspace, not a single elected official, in either political party, is raising the critical question of how we can ensure that the productivity gains of the Information Age are shared equitably.

In the past, when new technology increased productivity—such as in the 1920s when oil and electricity replaced coal- and steam-powered plants—American workers organized collectively to demand a shorter workweek and better pay and benefits. Today, employers are shortening not the workweek, but the workforce—effectively preventing millions of American workers from enjoying the benefits of the technology revolution.

THE DECLINE OF ORGANIZED LABOR IN THE INFORMATION AGE

Organized labor has been weakened by 40 years of automation, a decline in union membership, and a growing temp workforce that is difficult to organize. In meetings with union officials, I have found that they are universally reluctant to deal with the notion that mass labor—the very basis of trade unionism—will continue to decline and may even disappear altogether. Several union leaders confided to me off the record that the labor movement is in survival mode and trying desperately to prevent a rollback of legislation governing basic rights to organize. Union leaders cannot conceive that they may have to rethink their mission in order to accommodate a fundamental change in the nature of work. But the unions' continued reluctance to grapple with a technology revolution that might eliminate mass labor could spell their own elimination from American life over the next three or four decades.

Working women may hold the key to whether organized labor can reinvent itself in time to survive the Information Age. Women now make up about half of the U.S. workforce, and a majority of employed women provide half or more of their household's income.

In addition to holding down a 40-hour job, working women often manage the household as well. Significantly, nearly 44 percent of all employed women say they would prefer more time with their family to more money.

This is one reason many progressive labor leaders believe the rebirth of the American labor movement hinges on organizing women workers. The call for a 30-hour workweek is a powerful rallying cry that could unite trade unions, women's groups, parenting organizations, churches, and synagogues. Unfortunately, the voice of trade union women is not often heard inside the inner sanctum of the American Federation of Labor and Congress of Industrial Organizations (AFL-CIO) executive council. Of the 83 unions in the AFL-CIO, only one is headed by a woman.

The women's movement, trapped in struggles over abortion, discriminatory employment practices, and sexual harassment, has also failed to grasp the enormous opportunity brought on by the Information Age. Betty Friedan, the venerable founder of the modern women's movement and someone always a step or two ahead of the crowd, is convinced that the reduction of work hours offers a way to revitalize the women's movement, and take women's interests to the center of public policy discourse.

THE BENEFITS OF A SHORTER WORKWEEK

Of course, employers will argue that shortening the workweek is too costly and would threaten their ability to compete both domestically and abroad. That need not be so. Companies like Hewlett-Packard in France and BMW in Germany have reduced their workweek while continuing to pay workers at the same weekly rate. In return, the workers have agreed to work shifts. Management executives reason that, if they can operate the new high-tech plants on a 24-hour basis, they can double or triple productivity and thus afford to pay workers the same.

In France, government officials are playing with the idea of forgiving the payroll taxes for employers who voluntarily reduce their workweek. While the government will lose tax revenue, economists argue that fewer people will be on welfare, and the new workers will be taxpayers with purchasing power. Employers, workers, the economy, and the government all benefit.

In this country, generous tax credits could be extended to any company willing both to reduce its workweek voluntarily and implement a profit-sharing plan so that its employees will benefit directly from productivity gains.

MANY RECOGNIZE THE PROBLEM

The biggest surprise I've encountered in the fledgling debate over rethinking work has been the response of some business leaders. I have found genuine concern among a small but growing number of business executives over the critical question of what to do with the millions of people whose labor will be needed less, or not at all, in an increasingly automated age. Many executives have close friends who have been re-engineered out of a job—replaced by the new technologies of the Information Age. Others have had to take part in the painful process of letting employees go in order to optimize the bottom line. Some tell me they worry whether their own children will be able to find a job when they enter the high-tech labor market in a few years.

To be sure, I hear moans and groans from some corporate executives when I zero in on possible solutions—although there are also more than a few nods of agreement. But still, they are willing—even eager—to talk about these critical questions. They are hungry for engagement—the kind that has been absent in the public policy arena. Until now, politicians and economists have steadfastly refused to entertain a discussion of how we prepare for a new economic era characterized by the diminishing need for mass human labor. Until we have that conversation, the fear, anger, and frustration of millions of Americans are going to grow in intensity and become manifest through increasingly hostile and extreme social and political venues.

We are long overdue for public debate over the future of work and how to share the productivity gains of the Information Age. The 1996 election year offers the ideal time to begin talking with each other—both about our deep misgivings and our guarded hopes—as we journey into a new economic era.

> "We can do things to give [an]
> individual . . . the ability to land a
> job in this quote-unquote
> 'knowledge' economy, if and when
> their current job disappears."

THE INFORMATION REVOLUTION COULD CREATE JOBS

Dana G. Mead

Although many workers will be displaced by automation as the Information Revolution transforms the economy, willing employees can be retrained to fill the many new jobs that will be created, argues Dana G. Mead in the following viewpoint. Potential obstacles to retraining these workers, he contends, include high taxes that limit economic growth and labor union resistance to change. Mead is chairman and CEO of Tenneco, a global manufacturing company based in Greenwich, Connecticut. He is also the chairman of the National Association of Manufacturers in Washington, D.C. This viewpoint is excerpted from a speech delivered to the Economic Club of Detroit, Michigan, on May 15, 1996.

As you read, consider the following questions:

1. In Mead's opinion, why is economic growth so important for the transition to the knowledge economy?
2. According to Michael Cox and Richard Alm, cited by the author, in what ways are Americans better off now than in 1970?
3. What are the reasons for worker anxiety, in the author's view?

Reprinted from "Growth and the Road to Cyberspace," by Dana G. Mead, *Vital Speeches of the Day*, August 1, 1996, by permission of the author.

Today I'm going to talk about the transition of our economy to the Cyber-Age (or the knowledge economy as some label it) and some of the challenges we face on what I call the Road to Cyberspace.

As many of us have observed, there is sometimes a crossover between what's virtual and what's real.

By the virtual reality of the future—for example that we will be able, using our computers, to buy tickets for a trip to say, San Francisco, to book a meal at a Greek restaurant on a Saturday night, to look at the menu, the dining room, to read the food critic's review, pick a table, order ahead, even talk to your waiter—all of it in the virtual world of Cyberspace.

It sounds wonderful, but I'm an industrialist and also a realist.

I keep thinking someone has to manufacture the tables, the silverware and the napkins; someone has to produce the food; someone has to put the wine in the bottle, and someone has to get the product to the customer.

ECONOMIC PROBLEMS OF THE INFORMATION REVOLUTION

The transition to the Cyber-Age is proving to be a painful process.

The New York Times had a seven part series on it [in 1996]. And the [May/June 1996] issue of Foreign Affairs has the following on its cover: "The world may be moving inexorably toward one of those tragic moments that will lead historians to ask, why was nothing done in time?"

These articles and many like them point up the fact that our transition to the Cyber-Age holds huge potential for problems, big problems . . . economic insecurity, worker anxiety, social displacement and disruption . . . and the very damaging political repercussions that may well result.

This issue is not immune from political demagoguery—witness the [1996 presidential] campaign of Pat Buchanan, an old acquaintance of mine from my White House days.

The difficulty of this transition also has not escaped the fine political instincts of President Clinton. He [had] his [former] Labor Secretary, Robert Reich, out front as his point man basically polarizing the issue pitting managers against workers, investors against labor, government against corporations, larger corporations against small ones and so on.

And although the rhetoric has cooled a bit, organized labor, the media and others have picked up the themes and run with them.

This transition—in all of its ramifications—is perhaps the greatest domestic challenge we face in this country over the next decade. And it's a case of "how we get there" being just as important as "being there."

If we do not do it right, we are going to end up with all the things I've mentioned earlier—paying a hard political, economic and social price and causing historians to question "why we didn't do something."

Despite all the talk of our "virtual future," the Road to Cyberspace has to go through places like Newport News, Virginia, where ships are built; through Cozad, Nebraska, where they make shock absorbers . . . through Racine, Wisconsin, where they bolt tractors together . . . Counce, Tennessee, where they make linerboard, and of course, through this city of Detroit and its environs.

That's just an oblique way of saying that we must find some way to use the vast experience and talent of a "non-knowledge economy workforce" while we move to one with workers and managers who are "cyber-ready"—and to do so without losing our competitiveness.

THE IMPORTANCE OF ECONOMIC GROWTH

To get to the knowledge economy of the future is going to require huge resources, huge amounts of money—in people, time and effort.

That is why economic growth is so important to our transition. Unless we can achieve growth at high enough levels to generate the revenues that both government and business need—and it may not matter if it is government or the private sector that is spending the money—we won't be able to pay for the dislocations in our labor force . . . to pay for the training and retraining we need to equip our workforce with skills for jobs in the Cyber-Age . . . to establish effective safety nets for the inevitable dislocations and economic hardships.

We also have to pay for all the new Cyber-systems that will raise productivity—but which are already proving to be tremendously costly.

Has anybody here lately put in a new software system? Is there anybody here who thought it was cheap? Is there anybody here who does not believe that the next time is going to be even more expensive and complex? . . .

TECHNOLOGY'S EFFECT ON INFLATION

One of the things not being fully accounted for in the inflation debate is the result of increasing productivity—gains in output from what is known as "technology deepening."

What this means is, as we drive systems and innovations deeper and deeper into our organizations, we are getting a large boost in productivity—and often we don't even know it.

For example, Tenneco has increased productivity in one of our papermills by 9% in the last three years without adding a dollar of investment.

We have not hired more people to do it.

We have not inflated the cost of labor per ton of output. We have done it solely by improving our processes.

Globalization—and the fierce competition it has spawned—is another effective inflation fighter.

Most people do not understand how really global most businesses are. [In 1995] our Newport News Shipbuilding division signed a contract with a Greek shipping firm for four double-hulled tankers . . . basically an export item.

To help build those tankers, we probably have two thousand suppliers—small to medium size shops making parts for the ships. And if you asked them if they were exporters, most of them would probably say, no, they're suppliers to Newport News.

The intensity of global price competition is greater than many people think—it's not just the big multinationals, it's many of the firms who supply to them in countries across the world.

So much of what we are fighting in the halls of government and in the Federal Reserve is the misuse and misreading of economic data that don't take into account technology and globalization.

INFLATION RATES AND UNEMPLOYMENT

For example, the Federal Reserve and the rest of the low-growth crowd have been using an economic indicator called NAIRU—the awkward acronym for the even more awkward phrase it stands for: the non-accelerating inflation rate of unemployment.

Stated simply, NAIRU holds that when you go below a certain level of unemployment, the cost of labor will go up, triggering price increases on products and a spiral of inflation.

This has been the single most important indicator used by the [Federal Reserve] in monitoring inflation.

Of course, they get very upset with me, because I have been running around the country saying that NAIRU is to economics what the Nehru jacket is to fashion: Outdated.

I say that because the NAIRU has been systematically discredited.

People once thought the NAIRU was 6.1% unemployment. When unemployment got to 6%, the economists all said inflation is coming—sort of like Chicken Little, the sky is falling.

But we had no inflation. Then unemployment dropped to 5.8% in early 1995, and people thought, the sky really is falling this time. So the Fed jacked up interest rates.

But low and behold, there was still no inflation.

NAIRU is like predicting the End of the World (or the Red Sox winning the World Series): if you predict it long enough, you'll eventually be right.

My point is, if you're going to follow economic indicators, they've got to be the right indicators.

Another example of a dubious indicator used by the Fed is changes in inventories and absolute levels of inventories. Basically, when inventories are high, growth and inflation stay low. When they're low, growth and inflation go up. That's the conventional wisdom.

I played the skunk at the Sunday picnic the other day. I asked one of these economy watchers if he takes into consideration the fact that every business in America has tried to reduce its inventories . . . to shorten up its cycle time.

I explained, for instance, that in our auto parts business, we often build a focus plant right next to our customer's plant, so we can deliver parts for a particular platform in a matter of hours.

So I said to the inflation fighter, if you think that no inventory in the auto plant indicates runaway economic growth, you are using the wrong indicator.

THE NEW ECONOMY

My point is, nobody really understands the impact of the changes that business—particularly manufacturers—have brought to this economy.

What is the impact of massive increases in productivity? What is the impact of Just-in-Time inventory? What is the impact of reengineering—which is a fancy word for eliminating the things that customers won't pay for?

We have to begin to talk about these changes and their impact.

And it's going to be uncomfortable for everyone.

Uncomfortable for industrialists like me because, frankly, it conjures up the idea that part of this increased productivity may be from eliminating jobs.

We have to stand up to that issue. If our companies are to remain competitive in a global economy, we have to eliminate jobs that are no longer delivering value to customers . . . but at the same time, prepare people for jobs that are delivering value.

There is real irony in some of this jobs-and-growth debate. I was at a dinner in Washington a couple of weeks ago and a cabinet member got up and spoke proudly of the fact that the current administration has eliminated hundreds of thousands of government jobs.

Yet when it happens in the private sector, some government leaders call it corporate greed and labels CEOs "corporate killers."

So we have to take a very hard look at our economy . . . at the impact of the changes with an eye towards making this transition to the Cyber-Age a successful one.

To do that we have to focus on real issues, not phony ones that make good political rhetoric.

For example, the [former] Secretary of Labor (I seem to be picking on him a lot) talks about the decrease in real incomes for the average wage earner during the past twenty years. And he usually says it in the same breath as phrases like "corporate welfare" and "class warfare."

This is all very polarizing stuff, and it makes good sound bites—which partly explains why many Americans are confused and discouraged.

They might feel they're doing better than twenty years ago, but they're being told they're worse off.

WORKERS IN THE INFORMATION AGE

A report by Michael Cox and Richard Alm of the Federal Reserve Bank of Dallas puts some perspective on this paradox.

Alm and Cox used quality of life measures to compare 1970 and 1990. They found some interesting things.

I'll reel off a few of them:

The average size of a new home went from 1500 square feet to 2100 square feet.

People using computers rose from 100,000 to 76 million.

Households with VCRs went from zero to 67 million.

Attendance at symphonies and concerts, 13 million to 44 million.

The amount of time worked to buy gas for a 100-mile trip, from 49 minutes to 31 minutes.

People finishing high school: 52% to 78%.

People finishing college: 14% to 24%.

And life expectancy: 71 to 75 years.

These figures cast into doubt the idea that life has gotten worse for most Americans. And it warrants our taking a second look at the statistics so often cited by the doom and gloomers of this 7 to 10 percent decline in wages.

When you take into account things like the Consumer Price

Index's overstatement of inflation by one-half to one percent; the declining size of families; the growth of non-wage compensation like health care and pensions . . . most workers have seen compensation rise by up to 23%.

KNOWLEDGE WORKERS

A "knowledge economy" will likely develop in the United States during the decade of 2000–2010 as automation reduces the need for blue-collar and service workers.

Blue-collar workers should dwindle from 20% of the U.S. work force in 1995 to 10% or less within a decade or two. At the same time, the automation of office tasks will probably reduce the number of nonprofessional white-collar workers from about 40% at present to 20%–30%.

The remaining 60%–70% or so of the work force may then be composed of knowledge workers: skilled manufacturing teams, information system designers, managers, professionals, educators, scientists, and the like. Meanwhile, productivity, living standards, and the quality of life will soar to unprecedented levels.

William E. Halal, Futurist, November/December 1996.

You take a further look, and you see the biggest bite in real income has come from taxes. In 1955, taxes took an average 27% of household income; today the figure is 38%.

At the National Association of Manufacturers (NAM), we recommend a number of things the government can do to help this economy achieve higher growth: deficit reduction, tort and regulatory reform, paying down the national debt, many others.

But the first among equals is tax reform that will encourage investment over consumption. This will take real leadership because tax reform will not immediately produce growth.

And when it does kick in, it will probably first benefit upper income Americans more . . . which means there will be plenty of howling about the rich getting richer.

So what we at NAM have been suggesting is something that reaches well beyond tax reform, and that is a new covenant between business, labor, and government . . . a compact of mutual support to pursue pro-growth policies.

LABOR'S ROLE IN THE NEW ECONOMY

One of the ironies of the recent militancy of the labor movement is its timing, because American industry has finally figured out that within our plants, we have people with 35 or 40 years experience who know a hell of a lot more about how to run that corrugator or know how to run that paper machine than any of us wearing white shirts and suspenders.

For years we have not utilized that talent. Now that we're reaching out and doing so, we are confronting a huge backlash from unions.

Why? Well, if you think about it, when you bring labor and management together on a project, you are basically supplanting the union's conventional role . . . which was to communicate with their members, to decide what work they would do and to organize the work.

So they see the team concept as a direct threat to their existence. Making matters worse is the 1992 National Labor Relations Board ruling that supports a 1937 labor law that forming a labor/management team in a non-union facility is against the law.

We are being challenged in manufacturing facilities all over the United States, any time we put teams together—teams that are an absolute prerequisite to our staying competitive with the rest of the world.

That's part of what I mean by forging a new covenant.

Another part of that covenant has to do with the whole notion of gain sharing. This is a huge issue.

For years enlightened managers have tried to find ways to share company gains with unionized workers, and it has been very difficult to do so because it was often looked upon as a way to circumvent the contract—and their control.

REAL ANXIETIES FOR WORKERS

Now let me talk about worker anxiety.

Though there is a lot of misinformation and disinformation out there, the fact is, worker anxiety exists, and it's not a mirage.

There are reasons for anxiety, and here I depart from the party line, and believe it or not, I agree with the [former] Secretary of Labor.

It is a real problem. It includes things like people losing their jobs (and no new job prospects), their loss of benefits, and being unable to pay for their children's education.

Restructuring is going to continue—in whatever name you call it—and jobs will both be lost and changed.

The reason is the old "don't look back" syndrome—someone's gaining on you. For every business, there are a lot of someones across the globe catching up in places like India, China, Brazil and Slovenia. This is not likely to change.

One of the consequences of this intense competition is job

displacement. Twenty-five years ago, if you were a lathe operator, you had a skill . . . a marketable skill.

If you lost your job, the chances of your being out of work for very long were pretty low, because there were still jobs for lathe operators being created.

Now if you are a lathe operator, fifty years old, and you lose your job, the jobs that are being created are for people who can use distributive process control, or work in computer programming, or service robotics.

The skills of the old jobs being lost don't match the skills of the new jobs being created.

So we have to change our mindset. We can no longer guarantee a lifetime job.

We must begin to do what we can to guarantee lifetime employment by changing the skill set of people as they work for us.

We also have to be realistic. We cannot convert every welder at our shipyard to a computer jockey—that won't work.

But we can do things to give that individual a certain skill set that will increase the probability that he or she will have the ability to land a job in this quote-unquote "knowledge" economy, if and when their current job disappears.

Business, labor and government must cooperate to provide the training . . . and also pay for it. For its part, business needs to double what it spends . . . from 1.5% to 3%.

Meanwhile, workers—organized and unorganized—must be flexible. They must look upon their careers like opera singers—every 3 or 4 years developing a new repertoire . . . because a four-year-old repertoire is ancient history.

Like the opera singer, nobody is going to hire you for a new role unless you have learned the music. And there's more and more to learn with each passing year.

Providing Worker Training
Rather than Guaranteeing a Job

What are the ramifications of employment security as opposed to job security?

Well, for one thing, it means we are fast becoming a nation of job hoppers . . . which gets me to another area of cooperation: portability of benefits.

There is no reason we cannot develop a system of benefits people can take from job to job.

There is no reason why a worker should not take the equity built up in his or her pension fund to the next job.

There is no reason we cannot cooperate on benefits to help

educate our workers' children.

And there is no reason we can't give our employees a larger piece of the action in our companies—to align the owners', the managers' and the workers' interests.

When we brought our Case tractor division public two years ago, we gave every single employee—right down to the guy bolting tapping screws on a tractor—options on a hundred shares. Today those options are worth roughly $3,000.

Those are some of the things that we have to do to make this transition to the Cyber-Age—and then succeed when we get there.

But I'll remind you that the Road to Cyberspace won't be a smooth one. It has to pass through every factory, every union hall, every board room in the country—and also through Washington D.C. and all the state capitols.

This is not just an issue of "corporate responsibility," as many would like to call it, but of "national responsibility." It is going to take true leadership in the White House, Congress, business, and labor to make the transition successful.

And I think the jury is still out on whether we have that leadership in any one or all of these institutions . . . whether our leaders are ready to step up to the challenges and the risks that lie ahead.

> "America is only at the cusp of the telecom revolution and already there are ominous signs that poor neighborhoods and people of color are going to get stiffed."

THE INFORMATION REVOLUTION COULD CREATE INFORMATION HAVES AND HAVE-NOTS

Kim Nauer

The Telecommunications Act of 1996—which deregulates the telecommunications industry—could exclude low-income and minority communities from receiving new Information Age communication services, Kim Nauer argues in the following viewpoint. Because the act does not require the telecommunications industry to provide universal access to its services, she contends, telephone, Internet, and cable television companies are free to market exclusively to wealthy customers and ignore poor neighborhoods. Nauer is a senior editor of City Limits, a newsmagazine that chronicles New York City urban affairs.

As you read, consider the following questions:

1. According to Nauer, what does the Telecommunications Act of 1996 do?
2. What percentage of low-income schools provide students Internet access, according to the author?
3. What deal did public interest lawyers arrange with an Ohio phone company, according to Nauer?

Reprinted from "Holes in the Net," by Kim Nauer, City Limits, March 1996, by permission of City Limits.

I magine ...
    You're unemployed ...
Job listings, available on your television screen, allow you to apply the minute a
position becomes available.
You will.
And AT&T will bring it to you.
Unless, of course, you can't afford their new telecom service.
In which case you'll need a job ...
To afford AT&T ...
To have a hope of competing against those who are already wired with its
new tech ...
Click

THE NEWEST ELECTRONIC REVOLUTION

This is an uneasy moment for the nation.

With the President's signing of the Telecommunications Act of 1996, the news became official: the country is up to its neck in the next electronic revolution.

First telephone, then radio, then television: all had profound effects on the way people communicated and the ways in which they took part in America's culture and democracy. If the industry is to be believed, the next medium will be interactive, allowing people to communicate as they do over the phone; engaging, summoning the entertainment and commercial power of television, computers and the Internet; and educational, offering a wealth of new multimedia products integrating the best of both text and video.

Today, most homes have copper-wire hookups for their phones and, if they are cable television subscribers, they have wide-band coaxial cables. Interactive television and future computing will likely require something like digital fiber-optic cables or perhaps even wireless communication.

Federal and state policy makers must decide whether to encourage universal access to this technology, as President Clinton and public interest groups have called for. They must also decide if the technology is important enough to spend scarce public dollars retooling education and job training programs in poorer communities. Few doubt that this medium will profoundly affect the way Americans communicate with one another. But figuring out how low income and working-class people can participate in the revolution—and cash in—is another matter entirely.

The question cuts to the heart of a seminal debate: Will the technology eventually produce a new era of business and job opportunities? Or will it simply allow companies to shed more managerial and living-wage jobs? Most importantly, what can policy makers do today to ensure that telecommunications will strengthen the workforce rather than, as some predict, rip it apart along stark new lines of class and education?

In the wake of the Telecommunications Act—which largely deregulates the country's mammoth telephone, cable and broadcast companies—it's tempting to take a grim view. The law wipes out some 60 years of communications statutes laced with public interest safeguards, leaving a vacuum of uncertainty in their place. The hope among the law's supporters is that corporate competition will encourage innovation and keep prices low, allowing most Americans to benefit. The more sober among them concede, however, that this is unlikely without new regulations forcing companies to provide universal service and access for low income communities. And that, public interest advocates say, demands a long, hard fight.

STRUGGLING FOR EQUAL ACCESS AND EDUCATION

Just the same, there is a new school of organizers and education advocates running hundreds of small pilot programs nationwide who are certain the struggle is worthwhile. Typical is Robert McClintock, director of the Institute for Learning Technologies, whose New York–based nonprofit runs several experimental education programs using computers and the Internet to teach low income children research skills, critical thinking and teamwork—skills many believe will be the true job requirements of the next century. "This technology," he argues, "could be a tremendous equalizing force."

The Telecommunications Act requires companies to provide low-cost access to schools and libraries. Right now, he adds, thanks to all the Superhighway hype, people from the President down to school principals are talking seriously about investing in computers and Internet wiring. Moreover, the industry is already investing in education and community computing, if for no other reason than public relations. Suddenly there is a new tool that could, if accompanied by the right training, help students and their parents vault past all those outdated textbooks and neglected libraries. "This is a major opportunity—and a major risk," he maintains. "If the poorer neighborhoods get left behind this time, we will miss what may be the last major opportunity to address today's inequalities.". . .

Getting wired . . . will be easier said than done. America is only at the cusp of the telecom revolution and already there are ominous signs that poor neighborhoods and people of color are going to get stiffed.

According to a federal Education Department survey released in February 1996, an impressive one-half of the nation's public schools offer some kind of Internet access, whether in classrooms, labs, or libraries. However, just 31 percent of schools defined as low income—where more than 71 percent of students are eligible for free or reduced-price lunches—have Internet access. Compare that with survey results from schools in more affluent communities, where 62 percent, or two-thirds, have access to the net and the resources it provides.

Reprinted by permission of Mike Luckovich and Creators Syndicate.

At home, the picture is equally bleak. A November 1994 U.S. Census survey commissioned by Commerce Departments National Telecommunications and Information Administration found that one-fifth of poor urban residents didn't even have phones, let alone computers or modems. The percentage owning computers was at or under 20 percent among those earning less than $35,000 a year. Even among higher-earning city residents, only 35 percent of the families polled owned computers. The survey also found that only about half the people who bought computers chose to invest in a modem, the gateway to the technological revolution.

The Commerce Department did not poll largely white, suburban households to get comparison figures. However, the telecommunications industry, which tracks such trends closely, considers these affluent markets to be the most likely home to "the technologically advanced family." Married with 3.2 children, the typical "T.A.F.," according to a 1990 Yankee Group marketing survey, owns its own home with an average value of $118,000 and has an average annual income of nearly $60,000.

Problem is, T.A.F. is the family the telecommunications industry will seek to wire first, says Kofi Asiedu Ofori, counsel and lobbyist for the United Church of Christ, which has been a communications watchdog for minority communities since the early days of the civil rights movement.

Historically, telecommunications companies have opted to serve the wealthiest customers first, getting around to poor urban and rural communities last, Ofori explains. Most recently, he says, low income urban neighborhoods lagged far behind in access to cable TV hookups. While some in the industry and the media have dismissed this as a trivial issue—merely a distinction between "the haves and have-laters," as one *Wired* magazine editor put it—Ofori argues that wiring delays will create an all-too-familiar disadvantage to the poor communities.

Even if schools and libraries and community centers somehow arrange to get direct wiring or install other services that make up for the technology gap, the community will still be considered a backwater by those looking to start or relocate businesses, he says. Moreover, middle-class residents who add an element of stability to many poor neighborhoods would have one more incentive to leave if, indeed, this interactive revolution turns out to be as important as billed. Imagine, for example, having the money to buy a TV but lacking a local signal to make it work.

"I have no doubt that, yes, eventually these new communications services will be made available in low income neighborhoods, but it will be four, perhaps five years later," Ofori says. "The jump-start affluent communities get will make a big difference. Businesses will have already decided where they want to be located. Economically, the mold will have been cast.

"And that," he maintains, "is going to do nothing but exacerbate economic inequalities."

HISTORY OF THE TELECOMMUNICATIONS REFORM

The bill that became the Telecommunications Act of 1996 had been kicked around Washington in one form or another for more than a decade, and few deny that its passage was long overdue. The 111-page document consolidated a number of laws regulating the country's telephone, broadcast and cable companies and eliminated many of the outdated barriers preventing strategic corporate alliances and real competition from blooming in the new media. Industry leaders had been pushing the concept hard for years, pumping millions of dollars into Washington campaign coffers to drive home the point. Policy makers eventually allowed deregulation because, for the first time in communications history, they believed there was the potential for fierce competition between the various well-heeled conglomerates—as well as an army of entrepreneurial upstarts—to force innovation and keep prices in check.

But public interest advocates weren't convinced. They fought hard for provisions that would have required telecommunications companies to continue what is known as "universal service"—a traditional tenet of phone regulation that requires companies to serve those who may not be able to pay the full cost of service. Some good-government advocates also fought for language that would have forced telecommunications companies to arrange their cable-installing schedules to counter the "have-later" effect.

To its credit, the Clinton administration, led by Vice President Al Gore, stayed in the corner of public interest advocates long after they expected to be abandoned. Through the final months of intensive negotiations, the White House threatened a veto if the bill did not reflect at least some sense that the poorer communities would have a shot at equal access. The administration, clearly wanting to pass some piece of landmark legislation during an otherwise gridlocked budget year, ultimately backed the bill after congressional negotiators agreed, among other things, to insert an amendment requiring telecommunications companies to provide low-cost access to schools, libraries and rural hospitals.

THE TELECOMMUNICATIONS ACT DOES NOT ADDRESS ELECTRONIC RED-LINING

Both Congress and the administration, however, punted on universal service and the issue of electronic red-lining. The final bill included only vague language that acknowledged the problems and, at least in principle, outlawed them. But it is now up to the federal and state communications regulators to decide if the provisions have any teeth.

The deregulation law is also expected to result in price increases for many residential phone and cable customers. An intricate system of cross-subsidies that has long benefited residential phone customers will now suddenly be exposed to serious revision. "It was a bloodbath," sighs Audrie Krause, executive director of Computer Professionals for Social Responsibility. "This bill was bought and paid for by business interests."

The numbers support her contention. According to the Center for Media Education (CME), which tracked the congressional debate, telecommunications companies contributed more than $40 million in political action contributions to Congress over the last decade. In the first half of 1995 alone, tele-PACs [political action committees] gave some $2 million to congressional campaign funds, notes CME project coordinator Anthony Wright.

And that doesn't include the millions spent on personal donations, party contributions and the advertising that dominated the newspapers and television in the weeks before the final vote. "They spent millions," he says. "But it was an investment in billions."

So what is to be done to harness the forces of deregulation for the benefit of the nation's neglected communities? That's a problem with trying to make public policy for a new telecommunications age: No one really knows what's coming. "Our understanding of the questions we will face is, naturally, only partial, and generally conditioned by the only thing we have to go on—our past experiences," note authors Daniel Burstein and David Kline in their book *Road Warriors: Dreams and Nightmares Along the Information Highway.* They argue that neither the Clinton administration, which made access to technology a key part of its 1992 campaign platform, nor Newt Gingrich, who argues that Congress must lead the nation into the post-industrial Third Wave, has provided any real intellectual leadership on technological issues. Perhaps that's to be expected, they concede. "Considering the future itself is only partially visible, is it any surprise that many of the ideas about it are half-baked?"

PREDICTIONS ABOUT TECHNOLOGY AND THE FUTURE ECONOMY

It is a view from Plato's cave. Already there are conflicting predictions about the potential economic impact of telecommunications—and technology in general—on the workforce. Take just two examples that show how differently the technological age can be viewed. The first is cited in Burstein and Kline's book:

A March 1995 study commissioned by the Wharton Econometric Forecasting Associates (WEFA) Group, a respected econometric consulting firm, estimated that communications deregulation would spur a decade of remarkable growth, creating 3.4

million new jobs and a $298 billion worth of growth in the American economy.

A second, far grimmer perspective appears in an article by Jeremy Rifkin in the February 26, 1996, issue of *The Nation*: Author of *The End of Work*, Rifkin argues that technology, though not specifically telecommunications technology, will all but eliminate the world's manufacturing jobs. By the year 2020, Rifkin predicts, less than 2 percent of the entire global workforce will still be engaged in factory work. The service sector too would shed many of its jobs as computers take them over. About the only growing area will be the "knowledge sector"—communications—but its workers would have to be creative and thoughtful, an elite rather than a mass workforce.

These two seemingly disparate visions are not mutually exclusive. Economic growth can coincide, at least for a time, with major corporate downsizing. But how do activists prepare for this, knowing that the mass workforce is already ill-educated, underemployed and underexposed to the technology that Rifkin's elite "knowledge sector" will require? The answer for the moment is still access and education.

While it is true that the Telecommunications Act of 1996 represented a ringing victory for industry, public utility activists note that the passage of this law is just the beginning of a long and potentially productive fight.

It is inside the state legislatures, the courts and various federal and state regulatory boards that victories can be won as officials pore over the fine print—and the social implications—of the law. At the local level, testimony by activists and community residents is bound to generate significant interest and attention from public service regulators.

LOCAL ACTIVISM CAN PREVENT RED-LINING

There is already good reason to be hopeful. In Ohio, for example, public interest lawyers brokered a settlement with the local Baby Bell, Ameritech, after the company had been accused by the state public utility commission of charging excessive rates, says Ellis Jacobs, an attorney with the Legal Aid Society of Dayton. Ameritech, feeling the heat of new competition entering its market, was also asking the commission to cede its authority to review and control the company's profit margins, while retaining its ability to set rates. In hopes of settling the matter quickly, Ameritech struck a deal with the public interest parties. It reduced the rates for all residential customers, created the state's first-ever "life-line" program offering cheap phone service to the very poor, created an $18 million educational technology fund and contributed $2.2 million to set up 14 community computing centers statewide. . . .

ACTIVISTS CAN PRESS FOR EDUCATION AND ACCESS

Of course, universal service does not guarantee affordability to individual customers. Activists are also pressing for funding to support new community technology centers and educational services.

Already, notes CME's Wright, many public utility commissions are grappling with public service communications issues. As the telecommunications giants come before the commission seeking permission to expand or open new markets, community organizers can press for various types of quid pro quo. Early battles indicate that the companies, eager to protect their public image, can be convinced to fund a variety of technology access and education initiatives. "If you are interested, there are large opportunities for grassroots organizing," he says.

Finally, activists must keep in mind that pressing for education and access is only the first step in dealing with much larger issues to come. If it is true that computers and communication innovation will replace the bulk of today's living wage jobs, organizers better begin talking about new ways to ease the workforce into the post-industrial age.

The first step, however, is to make sure low income communities don't get left behind by the rest of America, yet again.

> "Have versus have-not, or zero-sum thinking, belongs to the Machine Age, not the Information Age."

THE INFORMATION REVOLUTION WILL NOT CREATE INFORMATION HAVES AND HAVE-NOTS

Steve Gibson

Many people have argued that the government should require the telecommunications industry to provide universal access to its services. Such requirements, some experts claim, would prevent the formation of a society of information haves and have-nots. In the following viewpoint, Steve Gibson maintains that such pressures on the telecommunications industry would limit its creative potential and stifle technological innovations in telephone, television, and Internet services. If the telecommunications industry is allowed to operate free of universal-service requirements, he contends, its services will eventually become affordable and attainable for everyone who wants them. Gibson is the executive director of the Bionomics Institute, a San Francisco–based organization that researches new theories on information age economics.

As you read, consider the following questions:

1. In Gibson's opinion, why is the Information Highway metaphor inadequate to describe the information network?
2. According to the author, how does the process of technological innovation bring new technology into lower-priced items?
3. According to Jeff Eisenach, quoted by the author, what is the problem with universal service requirements?

Reprinted from "Universal Disservice," by Steve Gibson, *Reason*, April 1995, by permission of the Reason Foundation.

Gutenberg's invention of the printing press cut the cost of copying information one thousand-fold, ultimately unleashing the scientific progress that created the Industrial Age and culminated some 400 years later as man landed on the moon. Since the invention of the microprocessor in 1971, by contrast, the cost of copying coded information already has dropped 10 million-fold.

If the looming changes brought forth from a technological innovation four orders of magnitude more powerful than the printing press leave you a bit confused, don't worry, Al Gore has the answer: the National Information Infrastructure, or NII. The administration's "Agenda for Action" begins with the promise of "a device that combine[s] a telephone, a TV, a camcorder, and a personal computer" that would bring "the best schools . . . vast resources of art, literature and science . . . health care . . . fulfilling employment . . . the latest movies . . . government benefits" and more. In sum, "whatever you need."

THE GOVERNMENT'S ROLE IN ENSURING FAIR ACCESS

By promising so much, Gore et al. creates an expectation that quickly tilts toward entitlement. If, as they suggest, the government must guarantee universal access to essential services, then who but the government can determine what constitutes "access," and what is "essential"? National Public Radio head Dell Lewis was among those named to advise the administration on what type of chicken belongs in every pot.

A major justification for government "guidance" in this $400 billion investment is fairness. Who among us, indeed, would want a society of "information haves and have-nots?" But the call for universal service is a red herring. It masks a fundamental mistrust of a process that will deeply reshape society and yet is almost entirely beyond government control. A process that is chaotic and self-organizing, utterly without a central plan. In other words, a market.

That this should cause some cognitive dissonance among the social engineering crowd is no surprise. David S. Bennahum, author of a book on cyberspace, notes in the New York Times that the Internet was created "mostly by accident" and worries about what kind of cyberspace we will get "if we surrender it to the vagaries of the market." The New Republic even goes so far as to castigate Wired, the magazine of the Information Age cognoscenti, for its "taint of contempt for the poor" and its "willful rootlessness and hyper-individualism" which "do little to minimize the class polarization and segregation that have always plagued the United States."

With the title "Anarchy, Chaos on the Internet Must End," an op-ed in the *San Francisco Chronicle* perhaps gets to the heart of the matter. Martha Siegel, author of *How to Make a Fortune on the Information Superhighway*, is appalled, rather than awed, by "an international computer web tying together about 30 million people [yet] governed by no one." She can scarcely imagine "the most powerful communication medium ever invented . . . left to the equivalent of mob rule." To her, the "need for firm direction is all too obvious." Firm direction, of course, means "the guiding hand" of the Federal Communications Commission (FCC).

That's not to say that there is not a very real danger of some being left behind. A 19th-century peasant, newly arrived in the big city, faced a skill and knowledge gap much narrower than will a 21st-century worker ignorant of the ways of the Infoweb. The very nature of the emerging information economy differs fundamentally from its industrial predecessor. While uncertainty comes hand in hand with rapid change, the ongoing universal-service debate misses four important truths.

Four Reasons Universal Service Is Unrealistic

First, Siegel is right. The Internet, the early progenitor of a 21st-century global Infoweb, is not governed by anyone. It is truly a self-organizing phenomenon, defined mainly by the simple rules, or protocols, which allow information to pass from one computer to another. Moreover, sometime soon if not already, nobody really knows for sure, the number of foreign Internet connections will outstrip those in the United States, making any attempts at national control futile.

Second, the "Information Superhighway" is anything but a highway. The paucity of our metaphor reflects the Machine Age mindset's inability to grasp an emerging, evolving, chaotic phenomenon. Unlike a planned, mapped, and relatively static highway, info-reality is a not-quite-seamless, organic web of Internet nodes, cellular modems, fax machines, CNN, GPS-equipped [Global Positioning System] delivery trucks, and 1,001 other microprocessor-enabled innovations. Together, they make manipulating, moving, and storing information cheap, time and distance immaterial, and hierarchy the quick route to organizational failure.

Third, information is fundamentally different from matter. If I mail my dad a copy of this article, I don't have that copy anymore. But if I e-mail him—and everyone else I know—I retain my copy. And my friends could do the same. Leaving the issue of intellectual property aside, we must remember that information is not material and carefully question statements that imply that it is. Unlike money, for example, information I have is not necessarily information that you have not. Have versus have-not, or zero-sum thinking, belongs to the Machine Age, not the Information Age.

Fourth, the idea of "convergence"—televisions, computers, and phones all merging into one, or vice versa—both will and will not occur. While increasing bandwidth [the capacity of optic fiber and satellite "pipes" to carry information] will allow once-separate technologies to overlap, there's no reason to expect one answer. Rather, we should anticipate many answers, as entrepreneurs create and fill niches based on consumer needs. Banks and bakeries do not have the same information infrastructure needs. Nor do all consumers. Bell Atlantic CEO Ray Smith identifies five different technologies that his company will (or might) use just to compete with cable companies for delivering video signals. In other words, there is no single twisted copper wire with matching black rotary phone that will be installed. Fortunately, as Peter Huber of the Manhattan Institute puts it, "the markets have already grasped this, even if the metaphor makers haven't." Nor have the policy makers, who rely on convergence to make their one-black-box-fits-all vision plausible.

GUARANTEED ACCESS VS. THE MARKET

That having been said, how do we get from the industrial here to the information there? Imagine that in 1895, some 13 years before the Model T, Al Gore's great-grandfather had correctly identified the potential importance of the new "horseless carriage" to future employment, and led the government push to ensure that we did not become a nation of "motorized transportation haves and have-nots." History provides an answer to this hypothetical question. Instead of the dizzying array of car classes that compose the U.S. automobile industry—essentially related, but separate, markets—we would be selecting among shades of black for our new Trabant.

By contrast, the process of technological innovation in a market environment is well documented. From jet engines to fiber optics, performance-conscious, price-insensitive consumers pay a premium for innovations, which drives unit production costs down the learning curve and brings the newer, better technology into ever lower price ranges. That's why anti-lock brakes are found in Chevys now, not just Cadillacs. That's why burgeoning cellular service, a luxury everywhere but L.A., enabled cellular service to arrive in certain rural homes not economically served by land lines, contributing to an increase in the percentage of homes with phones since the explicit cross-subsidies were phased out early in the 1990s.

The danger lies in deciding ahead of time that we all need anti-lock brakes in our car, or a videophone, or a certain set-top box on our TV, or any other single answer, because some technologies don't make the grade. The recent Japanese debacle with high-definition television shows how trying to guide, much less predict, technological innovation can leave consumers stuck with white elephant solutions.

EFFICIENT EQUIPMENT AND ECONOMIC GROWTH

By one estimate, since the Second World War 60 percent of U. S. economic growth has derived from the introduction of increasingly efficient equipment, the most important of which have been information machines. Around 1950 computers entered the economy, essentially as calculating devices, and the cost of crunching numbers plummeted. Between 1950 and 1980 the cost of a MIP (million instructions per second) fell between 27 and 50 percent *annually*. In the 1960s computers became labor-saving devices for storing, sorting and retrieving data, the cost of which probably fell at an annual rate of 25 to 30 percent between 1960 and 1985. But the labor-saving applications were job-creating: by 1980 there were 1.13 times as many information workers as production workers, up from 0.22 in 1900.

George F. Will, *Newsweek*, October 28, 1996.

When consumers are ready, new technology can, and does, spread with startling rapidity all by itself. Although the basic concept of facsimile machines had been around for decades, it took a microprocessor upgrade and consumer desire to bring "fax" into our vocabulary. From just 300,000 units in 1986, the installed facsimile base exploded to 10.7 million just six years later. Similar exponential growth patterns characterize the ongoing information revolution. According to Vinton Cerf, president of the Internet Society, if current growth rates continued, sometime early in the twenty-first century everyone in the world would have an Internet address.

Investors and early adopters pay for the innovations that fail, as well as the successful ones like fax. They should continue to do so, because progress comes from innovations unknowable in the time frame of Gore's vision: Apple Computer, Microsoft, and the personal computer (PC) itself have all existed for less than the estimated 20 years it would take to bring fiber-optic cable to every home in the United States. Undoubtedly, there is more than one goateed cyberpunk tinkering in his garage right now, looking for a better way. As long as there are geeks with a dollar to spend today on what will cost 50 cents tomorrow, just to be the first in their Usenet group to have it, new ideas will continue to germinate. Once government committees have the power to decide what society will need, the process of innovation will die.

MANDATING ACCESS TO INFORMATION WILL NOT WORK

To the level-playing-field crowd, letting some people have something all of us don't just isn't fair. As if free home access to Nexis and Dialog would miraculously provide jobs for the poor, these folks worry that "electronic red-lining" will keep such high-priced services only in the offices of law firms, investment banks, and other rich users, totally ignoring the rapid erosion of information services prices. Nothing short of mandating fiber-optic lines to every home will do. Even if a planned solution were technologically feasible, would this zero-sum, slice-of-the-information-pie policy work?

Not a chance, says Jeff Eisenach, president of the Progress & Freedom Foundation, a Washington think tank. "The problem in America today is not information have-nots, it's information want-nots," he notes. "Before we start putting a computer in every home, we have to create a culture in which people want the information a computer would provide."

He may be right. A television, today's prime source of information and entertainment, can be found in upwards of 99 percent of American homes, higher even than the 93 percent of homes with a phone. Without a hint of government subsidy—let alone a domestic producer—TV reaches more homes than telephones, despite six decades of sweeping universal telephone service policy courtesy of the Communications Act of 1934. Today, as computer price-to-performance ratios plunge, a used computer and modem can be had for prices equal to or less than a TV, with basic access to today's online world for about $9.00 per month. And, like virtually everything else in the high-tech arena, those prices are falling.

If "universal service" meant that buyers and sellers would be ensured access to each other (as with today's access to a variety of long-distance phone service providers) and that, perhaps, we would ask how best to get even one modem into every school (even without asking why they don't have them already), then

Washington would have made the first small steps in the right direction.

AN END TO RHETORIC

It's a positive sign that Vice President Gore's rhetoric seems to have evolved in its own right, away from the class-conscious, entitlement-creating "haves and have-nots" of early 1994 to at least the potential for deep reform. In January 1995, Gore suggested that what's needed is "the courage to throw out the regulated monopoly model that we've used for more than 60 years and instead create a truly competitive marketplace." But the rhetorical rubber has yet to meet the legislative road, and the potential for serious mischief, such as domestic-content requirements, remains.

More important, as long as the debate echoes with "on-ramps to the Information Superhighway" and other Machine Age images, Democrats and Republicans alike remain conceptually limited to policies that, at best, will produce a horseless carriage. Lacking an appropriate Information Age metaphor—economy as ecosystem—policy prescriptions inevitably ring with class consciousness and zero-sum thinking. Until the political mindset matches the organic reality of the Infoweb, the best we can hope for is a short waitlist for our e-Trabant.

PERIODICAL BIBLIOGRAPHY

The following articles have been selected to supplement the diverse views presented in this chapter. Addresses are provided for periodicals not indexed in the *Readers' Guide to Periodical Literature*, the *Alternative Press Index*, the *Social Sciences Index*, or the *Index to Legal Periodicals and Books*.

Craig Cox	"The Nerd Barons," *Utne Reader*, November/December 1996.
Damon Darlin	"He Wants Your Eyeballs," *Forbes*, June 16, 1997.
Bill Gates and Michael Dertouzos	"Friction-Free Capitalism and Electronic Bulldozers," *New Perspectives Quarterly*, Spring 1997.
William E. Halal	"The Rise of the Knowledge Entrepreneur," *Futurist*, November/December 1996.
Michael Hammer	"Reversing the Industrial Revolution," *Forbes ASAP*, December 2, 1996.
Mark Hodges	"Is Web Business Good Business?" *Technology Review*, August/September 1997.
Kevin Kelly	"New Rules for the New Economy: Twelve Dependable Principles," *Wired*, September 1997. Available from 520 Third St., 4th Fl., San Francisco, CA 94107.
Michael J. Mandel	"The Triumph of the New Economy," *Business Week*, December 30, 1996.
Peter Meiksins	"Work, New Technology, and Capitalism," *Monthly Review*, July/August 1996.
Andrew Ross	"Dividing Our Time: The Other Side of the Net," *New Perspectives Quarterly*, Winter 1997.
Amy Saltzman	"You, Inc.," *U.S. News & World Report*, October 28, 1996.
Andrew L. Shapiro	"Total Access," *Nation*, January 6, 1997.
David Pearce Snyder	"The Revolution in the Workplace: What's Happening to Our Jobs?" *Futurist*, March/April 1996.

Hal R. Varian   "The Information Economy," *Scientific American*,
                       September 1995.

George F. Will   "Healthy Inequality," *Newsweek*, October 28,
                       1996.

Rich Willis   "New Math: One Plus One Equals Four," *Forbes
                       ASAP*, December 2, 1996.

Shoshana Zuboff   "The Emperor's New Workplace," *Scientific
                       American*, September 1995.

CHAPTER 4

ARE RIGHTS THREATENED IN THE INFORMATION AGE?

Chapter Preface

The Communications Decency Act (CDA), signed into law by Bill Clinton in February 1996, attempted to bar indecent speech and pornographic images from the Internet to protect minors from viewing such material. Supporters of the CDA maintained that the proliferation of computers and the lack of regulation on computer networks make it too easy for children to access offensive and obscene material. Moreover, they argued, minors often encounter Internet pornography accidentally. As reported in the March 17, 1997, *Washington Post*, for example, a seventh-grader unwittingly accessed pornography by using the search words "Little Women" while gathering information for a book report on a novel by Louisa May Alcott. In light of such incidents, CDA proponents claimed that society has a right and a duty to protect its youth from offensive and potentially harmful material by passing laws to restrict indecent speech and images in public arenas. They pointed out, for instance, that restrictions are already placed on the media: radio broadcasters cannot use offensive language and network television cannot air explicit sex and nudity. These regulations on indecent material should also be applicable to the Internet, CDA supporters contended.

In June 1997, however, the CDA was struck down by the U.S. Supreme Court. Justice John Paul Stevens asserted that the CDA violates the First Amendment because it "effectively suppresses a large amount of speech that adults have a constitutional right to receive and to address to one another." Civil liberties advocates and computer-related businesses supported the Supreme Court decision, contending that governments should not have the authority to decide what kind of Internet material is appropriate for individuals and their children. Such government restrictions, they argue, could have censored serious discussions about birth control practices, information on the consequences of rape, and some classic works of literature and art. Rather than enforcing governmental limitations on Web material to protect minors, CDA critics maintain that parents should regulate their children's Internet use. Various software programs that block out unsuitable Internet content are readily available for parental monitoring purposes, civil liberties advocates point out.

Concerns about Web content, privacy rights, and copyright protections continue to fuel debate as new information technologies become increasingly available. The authors in the following chapter offer several perspectives on rights in the information age.

> "The information age has brought us many wonders, but it has also made possible an unprecedented level of recordkeeping and high-tech snooping into the lives of others."

THE RIGHT TO PRIVACY IS THREATENED IN THE INFORMATION AGE

Reed Karaim

Because many confidential records are stored on computerized databases that are not secure, people can use computer networks to obtain private information about others, Reed Karaim asserts in the following viewpoint. Marketing companies, in particular, he maintains, collect, buy, and sell such personal information without approval. It is lamentable, he contends, that most people blithely accept the loss of privacy that new technologies have produced. Karaim is a reporter and freelance writer.

As you read, consider the following questions:

1. According to John Kasson, cited by Karaim, where did the traditional notion of privacy originate?
2. In the author's opinion, for what purpose do the World Wide Web and other networks exist?
3. Why did Ram Avrahami sue U.S. News & World Report, according to Karaim?

Reprinted from "The Invasion of Privacy," by Reed Karaim, Civilization, October/November 1996, by permission of the author and Civilization.

I met the digital version of my life in a small, cluttered office in downtown Washington. A woman I had just been introduced to clicked a few keys on her computer and a remarkable summary of my existence flickered across the screen.

In short order, she found the places I had lived for the last 10 years, the names of my neighbors, an accurate estimate of my household income, my age, height, weight, eye color, Social Security number, my wife's name, evidence of my past divorce. Confidential (I thought) information about my mortgage appeared in minutes, as did a detailed description of my home, right down to the number of bathrooms and fireplaces and the type of siding. The bankruptcy of a relative surfaced, but so did a reassuring indication that my electronic self has not acquired a criminal record, at least in my home state, Virginia.

PERSONAL INFORMATION ON THE NET

Everything that Betsy Wiramidjaja, a researcher for the Investigative Group, Inc., found about me was in databases that can be accessed for as little as $1.50 a minute or $30 a month. The information is available to businesses and the general public through several different providers. Had I turned to a slightly less ethical company willing to probe credit and marketing data, much more—from my bank balances to my personal interests—could have appeared on the screen.

I'd come to the offices of IGI, a heavyweight investigative firm, for a firsthand look at the data that floats in the virtual ether about almost every one of us. In a time of talk shows, minicams and thousand-gigabit databases, my concern was an old-fashioned, faintly Victorian notion: the question of privacy.

The information age has brought us many wonders, but it has also made possible an unprecedented level of recordkeeping and high-tech snooping into the lives of others. While we dazzle ourselves in virtual worlds and strange new digital communities that stretch around the globe, it's easy to forget that the same technology that connects us can keep track of us as never before.

"Privacy is to the information economy what environmental protection was to the industrial economy," says Marc Rotenberg, director of the Electronic Privacy Information Center, a Washington-based advocacy group. "This new economy is incredibly productive and important, but there are costs. We are now confronting these costs."

The price is more than just the unease of realizing that your mortgage or the number of bathrooms in your home has become a matter of public record. Both government and corporate

America have found the new technology irresistible. In their embrace of the latest high-tech tools, they are shifting the boundary between the private and the public spheres in ways that challenge our fundamental notion of what part of one's life belongs to oneself. . . .

THE HISTORY OF PRIVACY

The history of privacy is a history of the modern West. The notion hardly exists in many tribal cultures and has little significance in the heavily populated nations of the Far East. Even in Western societies, the notion of an inviolable space into which others should not intrude is a recent phenomenon: Diaries from the 17th century and earlier recount the commonplace of sharing beds with strangers while traveling, bodily functions casually displayed, and a ribald lewdness that would be right at home on MTV.

John Kasson, a historian of social customs, says our traditional notions of privacy largely developed in reaction to the crush of cities in the industrial age. The crowded, fluid nature of places like London and New York pushed people of all classes together and began to dissolve the social order. In defense, the Victorians established an elaborate perimeter of ritual courtesies, codes of behaviors and social taboos to guard personal space. They tried to build a temple of the self too sacred for others to violate.

So also came a world constructed around ever-deepening layers of intimacy. There were streets and squares and other public spaces, in which one was expected to appear neat and clean and act with decorum. There was the neighborhood, in which a more casual, less affected appearance was acceptable, but emotion often remained hidden under a veil of sociability. There was the home, in which certain courtesies, such as offering food and drink, became paramount. There was the family gathered around the dinner table. There was the husband and wife in bed at day's end. There was, finally, the private echo chamber of the mind with its Freudian cellar full of Gothic desires and fantasies.

Kenneth Gergen, a professor of psychology at Swarthmore College, describes the notion that the "self" was found in the last, inmost place as the "romantic idea of the deep interior." In his book The Saturated Self, Gergen notes that this idea still holds great sway. "The notion is related to a sense of deep privacy," he says, "of having a place within one's self which is not open to the public."

But if we long for privacy in an increasingly complex and hectic world, the irony is that the nature of that world makes it ever-more necessary for strangers to keep track of us. In a society where the family doctor has been replaced by the multistate health-care corporation, for example, detailed medical records are a necessity. Accurate credit and bank information have become essential to a highly mobile population. We claim to hate "junk mail," but the catalogs and subscription notices targeted to our lifestyle result in convenient purchases more often than we admit, or they wouldn't be sent.

TECHNOLOGY AND THE LOSS OF PRIVACY

The fax machine, call waiting, e-mail and cellular phones have all brought, along with their obvious benefits, further encroachments into that small part of the universe into which we can retreat in solitude. But these intrusions pale when compared to the redefinition of public and private space wrought by the computer. It's not simply that computers make it easier to compile vast amounts of information on all of us, but that through the creation of virtual, on-line worlds, they create another reality in fundamental opposition to the idea of privacy. The World Wide Web and other networks exist to *share*. That is their reason for being. It's hardly surprising that the electronic trail that Betsy Wiramidjaja found so easily for me is out there somewhere for almost every one of us.

"When we first started, I remember being staggered by the amount of information that we were able to obtain on people in a matter of seconds. We probably have 50 or 60 databases we can access," says Terry Lenzner, who heads the Investigative Group, Inc. "There's a huge amount of information now in the public record." Most of us probably are dimly aware that our names and spending habits are sold on computerized marketing lists. (How else to explain the flood of junk mail that follows every significant event in our lives, from buying a house to having a child?) Most of us also recognize that personal material is alive in government and medical computers. We reassure ourselves with the belief that the most sensitive information—our tax records, for example—is securely held.

Our faith may be naive. In his book *Privacy for Sale*, Jeffrey Rothfeder, a former *Business Week* editor, interviewed "information brokers" who would provide a person's tax record for the last three years for a modest $550. The brokers could obtain almost anything stored in a computer somewhere: bank balances, credit-card information, even a record of all telephone calls made from a number for the last 60 days. The cost for the last service was only $200.

Even the Internal Revenue Service (IRS), it turns out, is hardly the secure vault we would like to believe it to be. In 1993, nearly 470 IRS employees were investigated or disciplined for browsing through the tax records of neighbors, acquaintances and celebrities, or for creating fraudulent tax refunds. A congressional investigation four years earlier found similar problems. In 1995 two IRS employees were charged with using their access to the service's computer system to obtain tax records for political reasons. One examiner was collecting information on the primary opponent of a U.S. House member. The other, Richard W. Czubinski, was indicted for illegally investigating several political aides in the Boston area. Czubinski was involved in the white-supremacist movement, and investigators believe he also was seeking tax information on right-wing associates he suspected of being government informers. . . .

Marketing and Ownership of Personal Information

The last great repositories of information about us, of course, are the marketing databases used by companies to track what we like to buy, eat, read, watch and do in our spare time. These databases cover even the very young. Metromail, for example, maintains basic information such as ages and addresses on 32 million children nationwide. Reportedly, a subcontractor for the company once employed prison inmates to work on its databases.

How hard is the information to obtain? In 1996, a Los Angeles television reporter put Metromail to the test when she sent them a money order for $277, using the name Richard Allen Davis. Davis is the man who was convicted in the 1993 kidnapping and murder of 12-year-old Polly Klaas. Nonetheless, Metromail sent the reporter a list of 5,000 children's names, ages, phone numbers and addresses—no questions asked.

Before long, it may become even easier to get your hands on such sensitive data. In 1990 a major software firm and Equifax, one of the nation's credit-report firms, hatched a joint venture that would have put personal information about more than 100 million citizens on a set of CD-ROM discs for sale. (Want a list of wealthy women living alone in a neighborhood? You would have been able to run a search.) The companies abandoned the idea in the face of intense criticism. But does anyone familiar with the history of commerce doubt it will return?

The idea of companies making money by selling information about us without our knowledge or consent is strange, when you think about it. Ram Avrahami of Arlington, Virginia, has thought about it a lot, and, in a lawsuit that could dramatically affect the direct-marketing industry, he is suing U.S. *News & World Report* for selling his name as part of a marketing list. (Many magazines rent subscriber lists to other magazines and marketing firms, as well as obtain such lists to identify prospective subscribers.)

"Two-Way Mirror"

©1997 Kirk Anderson. Reprinted with permission.

Avrahami's suit is based on a Virginia law that says others cannot use a person's "name, portrait or picture" in trade without obtaining permission. Avrahami took action after getting fed up with junk mail and telephone solicitations. "It was intrusive enough, repetitive enough, annoying enough that it caused me to think," he says. The more Avrahami pondered what was happening, the more it bothered him. Somewhere out there, information about him, including his name, was being traded like a pork-belly future. The key to Avrahami's suit is the principle that he is entitled to share any financial rewards that come from selling his name. Although a Virginia circuit court ruled against him in June 1996, he has decided to appeal his case to the state supreme court. Avrahami knows any payment would be minuscule but says his goal is to remove the financial incentive for companies to sell names back and forth without permission. "As long as they have the commercial incentive," he says, "some of my privacy will be stolen."

Direct marketing is only one example of the relentless creep of consumer culture into every corner of our lives, an invasion of privacy greatly aided by information-age technology. The on-slaught of advertising and sales pitches has already overrun the Internet. Junk e-mail could be the next great marketing tool: There are proposals to allow advertisers to clog your home computer's memory with the same stuff that clogs your mailbox.

PERSONAL INFORMATION AND POPULAR CULTURE

We live in an age consumed, in the words of the French philosopher Jean Baudrillard, with "the ecstasy of communication." Americans line up to reveal their darkest secrets, their most intimate moments, on talk shows. If Socrates were alive today, he'd have to change his famous aphorism: The unexposed life, he would conclude, is not worth living. So it may seem absurd to worry that privacy is endangered because somebody has our Social Security number and our purchases from Land's End on file.

But the battle is not about how much privacy some of us choose to do without: It's about the freedom to choose. "It's really about people's ability to move back and forth between a public world and a private world," says Marc Rotenberg.

There are those enamored with the onrush of technology, who believe that the best of all worlds is one in which everyone can peer into everyone else's life. Science writer Charles Platt concluded an article on electronic surveillance in *Wired* with this observation: "Personally, I look forward to a time when no one will be exempt from surveillance. So long as corporations, governments, and citizens are equally vulnerable, lack of privacy will be the ultimate equalizer."

Prophets of every revolution have always believed in remaking humankind, and the idea of complete openness has a kind of idealistic appeal. But it flies in the face of history. There is no indication that the powerful would be any more willing to disrobe and accept equality with the powerless than they have ever been. There is no indication that a world without privacy would protect the unpopular, dissenters, those in the minority.

Privacy advocates point out that there is no inherent reason some of the technology of the information age cannot be used actually to *enhance* privacy. Encryption programs, for example, can make computer and telephone communications as secure as whispering in someone's ear—more secure, in fact, since the best bugs these days pick up even whispers. "Technology can be used both to promote privacy and invade privacy," says Rotenberg. "The old equation—the more technology, the less privacy—is breaking down. We're heading toward a real choice between technologies of privacy and technologies of surveillance.". . .

Through much of this century we have been haunted by totalitarian fantasies in which our lives are stolen from us by all-powerful forces. The assault on privacy, however, ends up being more a matter of convenience, inattention and the thoughtless embrace of technology than a conspiracy by unseen overlords. There is no Big Brother. But in our childlike craving for security, we are creating a world in which Big Brother—like Jean-Paul Sartre's idea of hell—is other people.

The change is no less profound or troubling because it comes half-willingly and in dribs and drabs. It is now taken for granted that our finances, political predisposition, consumer preferences, even our sexual habits are a legitimate matter of public record—ideas that would have been considered a vision straight out of George Orwell's 1984 not that long ago.

We also have come to accept the idea that our desires and identity are just more commodities to be sold on the infobahn. It's hard not to cheer for Ram Avrahami as he tries to regain control of how his name is used by others. His battle is, in one sense, the battle all of us face as technology nibbles away at the private space in our lives.

The era of the million-gigabit memory, the microchip and the minicam has given us a world turned inside out, but this could be its ultimate paradox: In the information age, the information that truly matters is still the information you can keep to yourself.

"Simple loss of privacy is not the real problem underlying all the tossing and turning we're going through over the openness the Internet has thrust upon us."

THE RIGHT TO PRIVACY IS NOT THREATENED IN THE INFORMATION AGE

Jeffrey Obser

In the following viewpoint, Jeffrey Obser argues that Americans' demand for personal conveniences necessitates the computerized databases that some people worry will invade their privacy. The quest for privacy in modern life has resulted in individual isolation, he contends, making detailed recordkeeping and surveillance necessary to establish personal credit and other amenities. Obser is an intern at *HotWired*, an online magazine.

As you read, consider the following questions:
1. In Obser's opinion, what are two effects of the isolated existence most people lead in modern life?
2. According to James Wheaton, quoted by the author, why is it wrong for the government to restrict access to databases?
3. What is a legitimate issue of information privacy, in the author's view?

Reprinted from "Privacy Is the Problem, Not the Solution," by Jeffrey Obser, *Salon*, June 26, 1997, by permission of *Salon*, an online magazine at www.salonmagazine.com.

I wonder what Richard Nixon would have thought of the recently concluded [June 1997] Federal Trade Commission (FTC) hearings on privacy in the datasphere. After all, Nixon suffered the most humiliating privacy loss ever. Surely he could empathize with all the people who are upset that strangers can find dossiers about them on the World Wide Web, or that their personal information has become an unregulated commodity floating through distant databases. He was as shocked and confused as we are that a convenient new communications technology—in his case, audiotape—would turn around and tattle on him. And, just like us, he reacted by demanding more privacy.

It mystifies us that the man thought he could have it both ways—record everything, and get away with everything. But curiously, it mystifies nobody that we all expect to talk freely and shop with convenience through electronic networks without establishing some sort of reputation for ourselves. In conditions of the utmost anonymity, living in "communities" where neighbors don't talk to one another, we expect, as Nixon did, to be trusted. And we are outraged to find that it's not possible, and they're subpoenaing our tapes on Capitol Hill. Why, we ask, does anyone need to know all this stuff about me?

PRIVACY MAY BE A PROBLEM

The exploitation of personal data that the FTC hearings took up is plainly a serious problem. But nobody wants to admit that privacy itself may really be that problem's root cause rather than its antidote.

Modern life allows us an unprecedented level of physical privacy in real time and space. This isolated existence not only feeds our paranoia but necessitates the electronic record keeping that enables us to deal all day with total strangers. As the scale of interactions and commerce broadens across the Web, the complexity of that record keeping promises only to deepen.

Want to buy gas on credit? Easy! Even easier than the times when the mechanic down the street knew you personally. The difference is that now, the pump will know your name, a distant computer will make a record and the fellow behind the bulletproof glass won't give a damn. He has privacy, you have privacy. Everyone happy?

It's no coincidence that the jurist Louis Brandeis wrote his often-cited, groundbreaking "right to be let alone" privacy screed in 1890, just when the close-knit scrutiny of real villages began to give way to the anonymity of urban life. People took privacy for granted until then; in the days before databases, it was not an abstract quality. One's bedroom or backyard were either private or they weren't—and one's reputation was rarely more permanent or widespread than the memory banks of the people one dealt with personally.

Over the last 50 years, our journey into suburbs and cars and flickering TV nighttimes behind barred windows has given us extraordinary seclusion in our personal and home lives. And yet we've only felt more insecure. Only 34 percent of Americans polled by the Louis Harris firm expressed concern about personal privacy in 1970. By 1995, the figure was up to 80 percent.

What happened? This growing concern doesn't indicate a simple increase in how much we value privacy, any more than the soaring number of lawyers in the U.S. means we value justice more. Instead, it's a fearful reaction to the collapse of trust in our culture.

TECHNOLOGICAL INNOVATIONS AND THE LOSS OF PRIVACY

In *The Naked Society* (1964), Vance Packard trembled at the 20th century innovations that were draining American life of privacy and autonomy: social control by large, impersonal employers; pressure on companies to scrutinize customer choices in a sophisticated manner in order to compete for market share; galloping advances in electronic technology; and the McCarthy-era adoption of a pervasive top-security mentality in both government and business.

Nearly a decade later, at the dawn of computerized record keeping, James B. Rule pointed out in *Private Lives and Public Surveillance* (1973) that the transition to a society of mobile strangers didn't necessarily increase surveillance—the prying eyes of small-town neighbors are, he felt, in most cases worse. But it did lead to more *centralized* surveillance—out of sight and, for practical purposes, beyond the control of the individual.

By 1993, in the book *The Costs of Privacy*, Steven L. Nock attacked privacy itself as the problematic result of systemic social separation. "Privacy grows as the number of strangers grows," Nock wrote. "And since strangers tend to not have reputations, there will be more surveillance when there are more strangers. Privacy is one consequence, or cost, of growing numbers of strangers. Surveillance is one consequence, or cost, of privacy."

Nock called credit cards, those handy generators of much of the personal data we've lost control over, "portable reputations." In the era of the Internet, cheap computing and an increasingly global economy, those portable reputations record more and more of our activities, and more and more strangers and institutions demand them from us. The trends toward economic consolidation, less face-to-face accountability in our public lives and faster computing will exert great pressure for ever more elaborate identification and credentialing schemes. The spread of the use of the social security number to 60 government agencies is one result of this pressure. Retina and thumbprint scans, already in pilot testing, will be the next.

We can complain all we want about Big Brother, but when we wrested our reputations from human memory and turned them over to far less judgmental computer circuits and phone lines—vanquishing those nasty old village snoops who might keep us from living out our hearts' desires—reputation remained as important as ever. The difference is that even as we have downplayed its significance—whether out of honest egalitarianism or excessive individualism—we have consigned it to the banal, impersonal testing ground of supermarket checkout stands and pre-employment background checks.

ARE PRIVACY LAWS NEEDED?

The only thing a computer ever asks is: Are you approved, or not? And everyone from medical insurers to prospective employers to creditors views us as a potential threat until our data prove otherwise. Setting up new privacy regulations isn't going to alleviate this pressure; it may only lead to more elaborate credentials and invasive identifiers for individuals, and increased secrecy for the institutions that manage our reputations.

Privacy, particularly when enshrined in law, can protect the corrupt and malign as well as the good and upstanding. But the bulk of breathless newspaper reports issuing forth on this issue since 1996 have almost universally ignored this, instead focusing on the hypothetical risks of baddies out there finding out where Joe Consumer lives and (gasp!) what his children's names are. Most have taken the same grave, utterly simplistic angle: Privacy good. Stalkers bad. Internet dangerous. Call Congressman. All have invariably repeated the same shopworn Top 10 privacy-violation horror stories, mostly hypothetical and mostly based on the absurdity of having to hide out from one's Health Maintenance Organization (HMO), spoon-fed to hungry reporters by a small group of widely quoted privacy activists. James Wheaton, senior counsel of the First Amendment Project, an Oakland, Calif., group trying to protect and expand the Freedom of Information Act, laments "enormous imprecision" in the concerns raised by some of these activists.

By giving government officials the power to deny public-records access to anyone without credentials (i.e. the little guy), Wheaton says, "the privacy activists may inadvertently be helping the moneyed interests and doing nothing for greater security." Even with their good intentions and a laudable commitment to civil liberties, the professional privacy advocates have little besides fear as a selling point—fear of the stalker, the fraud perpetrator, the government agency run amok. But the fear and paranoia that have become so entrenched in the public mind are the primary cause of all this high-tech surveillance in the first place, because nobody wants to deal with anybody in person any more.

FEARS ABOUT PRIVACY INVASION ARE EXAGGERATED

Anyone who has ventured onto the World Wide Web knows the nightmare scenario.

It's an Orwellian world of privacy invasion and subliminal behavior control. It's a world in which computers log your every move on the Internet, distilling your behavior into individual dossiers that diabolical marketers then use to tailor their pitches to you, the unwitting consumer.

So, should you be scared?

It's too soon to tell whether the nightmare scenario will become a reality—online marketers are only now beginning to put controversial tracking tools to work. And few would argue vigilance isn't needed. But there are reasons to believe that the future may not be quite as frightening as some suggest.

For one thing, millions of consumers already divulge information about themselves through price scanners, automated-teller machines, credit cards and all the other means of electronic commerce considered essential. In addition, Internet tracking could actually be convenient for consumers, filtering out all the ads they don't want to see. And for those people who object to any tracking, software wizards are working to give them the ability to block Web intrusions.

Thomas E. Weber, *Wall Street Journal*, June 27, 1996.

Sure, there are legitimate issues of informational privacy, and at their best, the FTC hearings constructively aired them. Businesses that collect personal information from Web browsing should have some regulation against selling it, and anyone can see that companies compiling dossiers on every American are a threat to—Well, let's not bring up Hitler again. But the drumbeat of scare stories has focused too much attention on the Internet, even though nobody has explained how the Internet causes the problems in any direct or unique way. Credit-card fraud, costing literally billions of dollars in losses in recent years, was a problem as soon as credit cards were invented—and the Secret Service, which investigates computer crime, has no evidence to date that the resourceful credit-fraud rings have sought or needed help from the Internet.

COLLECTION OF INFORMATION BY THE GOVERNMENT

It's ironic that Americans are asking for privacy protection from the same government that has in the last few years expanded electronic surveillance beyond Richard Nixon's wildest dreams— always with an appeal to public fear and mistrust. Federal agencies are creating centralized databases to track every new job hire in the country (to catch illegal immigrants and deadbeat dads), to make sure that welfare recipients don't overstay their five years by changing states and to provide instant "terrorist" profiling to airport security agents. The country has not hesitated in the last few years to wipe out the civil liberties of whole swaths of the population in futile gropes for greater public security that's never attained.

But as soon as the most minute interest of upper-income people is threatened, Congress is shut down with phone calls, as it was during the Lexis-Nexis fiasco in the summer of 1995 and the Social Security Web site controversy in April 1996. Privacy is a vastly different issue to those whose names aren't on anyone's direct-mail list. Ask a homeless person what "privacy" means and the answer might involve a large appliance box. Once you're on the street, you're a reputation refugee—and no computer is ever going to approve your e-cash transaction.

THE NEED TO REEVALUATE TRUST

Simple loss of privacy is not the real problem underlying all the tossing and turning we're going through over the openness the Internet has thrust upon us. The entire experience of Internet use has total privacy as its point of departure—"meatspace" privacy, real-time anonymity, the kind that keeps anyone from knowing you're surfing the Web in your partner's underwear.

No, privacy is only part of the equation. The other part is the basic question of trust, that elusive property that we've all, in our hearts, given up on. This wide-ranging loss of our electronic virginity was well under way 20 years ago, but remained invisible until the Web forced us to confront it. We should be grateful for that. The arrival of the Global Village could be an opportunity to reevaluate our notions of trust and strangerhood. Maybe it will force us to.

Nixon's demands for privacy were ultimately fruitless and pathetic because there was no longer any trust to base that privacy on. He never understood that—and as privacy-loss hysteria begins to push laws through Congress that may do more harm than good, sadly, neither do we.

| "The interest in encouraging freedom of expression in a democratic society outweighs any theoretical but unproven benefit of censorship."

BANNING INDECENCY ON THE INTERNET IS UNCONSTITUTIONAL

John Paul Stevens

The Communications Decency Act (CDA) of 1996 sought to ban indecent speech and pornographic images from the Internet to protect minors from reading or viewing such material. Civil liberties advocates filed a lawsuit claiming that the CDA would also deny adults' rights to view pornography, a violation of the First Amendment protection of free speech. In the following viewpoint, excerpted from the Supreme Court decision striking down the CDA, John Paul Stevens supports the civil rights view, concluding that the CDA is unconstitutional. Stevens is a justice of the U.S. Supreme Court.

As you read, consider the following questions:

1. In Stevens's opinion, how does the vagueness of the Communications Decency Act (CDA) raise First Amendment concerns?
2. According to the author, how is adult conversation limited by prohibiting certain electronic transmissions that could be read by children?
3. What possible alternatives to the CDA could protect minors from obscene Internet material, according to Stevens?

Reprinted from the majority opinion of the Supreme Court of the United States, written by John Paul Stevens, in *Reno v. American Civil Liberties Union*, no. 96-511, June 1997.

A t issue is the constitutionality of two statutory provisions enacted to protect minors from "indecent" and "patently offensive" communications on the Internet. Notwithstanding the legitimacy and importance of the congressional goal of protecting children from harmful materials, we agree with the three-judge District Court [U.S. Court of Appeals for the Third Circuit] that the statute abridges "the freedom of speech" protected by the First Amendment. . . .

Regardless of whether the C.D.A. is so vague that it violates the Fifth Amendment, the many ambiguities concerning the scope of its coverage render it problematic for purposes of the First Amendment. For instance, each of the two parts of the C.D.A. uses a different linguistic form. The first uses the word "indecent," while the second speaks of material that "in context, depicts or describes, in terms patently offensive as measured by contemporary community standards, sexual or excretory activities or organs." Given the absence of a definition of either term, this difference in language will provoke uncertainty among speakers about how the two standards relate to each other and just what they mean. Could a speaker confidently assume that a serious discussion about birth control practices, homosexuality, . . . or the consequences of prison rape would not violate the C.D.A.? This uncertainty undermines the likelihood that the C.D.A. has been carefully tailored to the congressional goal of protecting minors from potentially harmful materials.

THE C.D.A. WOULD VIOLATE FREEDOM OF SPEECH

The vagueness of the C.D.A. is a matter of special concern for two reasons. First, the C.D.A. is a content-based regulation of speech. The vagueness of such a regulation raises special First Amendment concerns because of its obvious chilling effect on free speech. Second, the C.D.A. is a criminal statute. In addition to the opprobrium and stigma of a criminal conviction, the C.D.A. threatens violators with penalties including up to two years in prison for each act of violation. The severity of criminal sanctions may well cause speakers to remain silent rather than communicate even arguably unlawful words, ideas, and images. . . .

We are persuaded that the C.D.A. lacks the precision that the First Amendment requires when a statute regulates the content of speech. In order to deny minors access to potentially harmful speech, the C.D.A. effectively suppresses a large amount of speech that adults have a constitutional right to receive and to address to one another. That burden on adult speech is unacceptable if less restrictive alternatives would be at least as effective in achieving the legitimate purpose that the statute was enacted to serve.

In evaluating the free speech rights of adults, we have made it perfectly clear that "(s)exual expression which is indecent but not obscene is protected by the First Amendment.". . .

OVERSTEPPING FIRST AMENDMENT RIGHTS

Whatever the strength of the interest the government has demonstrated in preventing minors from accessing "indecent" and "patently offensive" material online, if the means it has chosen sweeps more broadly than necessary and thereby chills the expression of adults, it has overstepped onto rights protected by the First Amendment. Thus one of the factual issues before us was the likely effect of the Communications Decency Act (CDA) on the free availability of constitutionally protected material. A wealth of persuasive evidence, referred to in detail in the Findings of Fact, proved that it is either technologically impossible or economically prohibitive for many of the plaintiffs to comply with the CDA without seriously impeding their posting of online material which adults have a constitutional right to access.

Opinion of Dolores K. Slotiver, Third Circuit Court of Appeals, June 13, 1996.

It is true that we have repeatedly recognized the governmental interest in protecting children from harmful materials. But that interest does not justify an unnecessarily broad suppression of speech addressed to adults. As we have explained, the Government may not "reduc(e) the adult population . . . to . . . only what is fit for children." "(R)egardless of the strength of the government's interest" in protecting children, "(t)he level of discourse reaching a mailbox simply cannot be limited to that which would be suitable for a sandbox.". . .

PROTECTING CHILDREN DOES NOT OVERRIDE ALL CONCERNS

The District Court was correct to conclude that the C.D.A. effectively resembles the ban on "dial-a-porn" invalidated in *Sable Communications of California Inc. v. F.C.C.* In *Sable*, this Court rejected the argument that we should defer to the congressional judgment that nothing less than a total ban would be effective in preventing enterprising youngsters from gaining access to indecent communications. *Sable* thus made clear that the mere fact that a statutory regulation of speech was enacted for the important purpose of protecting children from exposure to sexually explicit material does not foreclose inquiry into its validity. As we pointed out last term [1995], that inquiry embodies an "over-arching commitment" to make sure that Congress has designed its statute to accomplish its purpose "without imposing an unnecessarily great restriction on speech.". . .

In arguing that the C.D.A. does not so diminish adult communication, the Government relies on the incorrect factual premise that prohibiting a transmission whenever it is known that one of its recipients is a minor would not interfere with adult-to-adult communication. The findings of the District Court make clear that this premise is untenable. Given the size of the potential audience for most messages, in the absence of a viable age verification process, the sender must be charged with knowing that one or more minors will likely view it. Knowledge that, for instance, one or more members of a 100-person chat group will be minor and therefore that it would be a crime to send the group an indecent message would surely burden communication among adults. The District Court found that at the time of trial existing technology did not include any effective method for a sender to prevent minors from obtaining access to its communications on the Internet without also denying access to adults. . . .

For the purposes of our decision, we need neither accept nor reject the Government's submission that the First Amendment does not forbid a blanket prohibition on all "indecent" and "patently offensive" messages communicated to a 17-year-old no matter how much value the message may contain and regardless of parental approval. It is at least clear that the strength of the Government's interest in protecting minors is not equally strong throughout the coverage of this broad statute. Under the C.D.A., a parent allowing her 17-year-old to use the family computer to obtain information on the Internet that she, in her parental judgment, deems appropriate could face a lengthy prison term. Similarly, a parent who sent his 17-year-old college freshman information on birth control via e-mail could be incarcerated even though neither he, his child, nor anyone in their home community, found the material "indecent" or "patently offensive," if the college town's community thought otherwise.

THE GOVERNMENT HAS NOT PRESENTED ALTERNATIVES

The breadth of this content-based restriction of speech imposes an especially heavy burden on the Government to explain why a less restrictive provision would not be as effective as the C.D.A. It has not done so. The arguments in this Court have referred to possible alternatives such as requiring that indecent material be "tagged" in a way that facilitates parental control of material coming into their homes, making exceptions for messages with artistic or educational value, providing some tolerance for parental choice, and regulating some portions of the Internet such as commercial Web sites differently than others, such as chat rooms. Particularly in the light of the absence of any detailed findings by the Congress, or even hearings addressing the special problems of the C.D.A., we are persuaded that the C.D.A. is not narrowly tailored if that requirement has any meaning at all. . . .

In this Court, though not in the District Court, the Government asserts that in addition to its interest in protecting children its "(e)qually significant" interest in fostering the growth of the Internet provides an independent basis for upholding the constitutionality of the C.D.A. The Government apparently assumes that the unregulated availability of "indecent" and "patently offensive" material on the Internet is driving countless citizens away from the medium because of the risk of exposing themselves or their children to harmful material.

We find this argument singularly unpersuasive. The dramatic expansion of this new marketplace of ideas contradicts the factual basis of this contention. The record demonstrates that the growth of the Internet has been and continues to be phenomenal. As a matter of constitutional tradition, in the absence of evidence to the contrary, we presume that governmental regulation of the content of speech is more likely to interfere with the free exchange of ideas than to encourage it. The interest in encouraging freedom of expression in a democratic society outweighs any theoretical but unproven benefit of censorship.

For the foregoing reasons, the judgment of the district court is affirmed.

| "Restricting what the adult may say to the minors in no way restricts the adult's ability to communicate with other adults."

RESTRICTION OF INDECENCY ON THE INTERNET CAN BE CONSTITUTIONAL

Sandra Day O'Connor

The Communications Decency Act (CDA) of 1996 sought to ban indecent speech and pornographic images from the Internet to keep minors from accessing such material. Many civil liberties advocates immediately sought to have the law declared a violation of the First Amendment right to free speech. In the following viewpoint, excerpted from a dissent to the Supreme Court decision striking down the CDA, Sandra Day O'Connor argues that the goal of barring children's access to indecent material is a legitimate role for government and that the CDA could have accomplished this goal in certain situations. If the CDA were tailored to achieve this narrower goal, she contends, it would be considered constitutional. O'Connor is a justice of the U.S. Supreme Court.

As you read, consider the following questions:

1. According to O'Connor, what criteria must a zoning law meet to be considered constitutionally valid?
2. How is the electronic world of the Internet fundamentally different from the physical world, in the author's opinion?
3. What is "gateway technology," according to the author?

Reprinted from the dissenting part of Sandra Day O'Connor's opinion in *Reno v. American Civil Liberties Union*, no. 96-511, June 1997.

I write separately to explain why I view the Communications Decency Act of 1996 (C.D.A.) as little more than an attempt by Congress to create "adult zones" on the Internet. Our precedent indicates that the creation of such zones can be constitutionally sound. Despite the soundness of its purpose, however, portions of the C.D.A. are unconstitutional because they stray from the blueprint our prior cases have developed for constructing a "zoning law" that passes constitutional muster. . . .

The creation of "adult zones" is by no means a novel concept. States have long denied minors access to certain establishments frequented by adults. States have also denied minors access to speech deemed to be "harmful to minors." The Court has previously sustained such zoning laws, but only if they respect the First Amendment rights of adults and minors. That is to say, a zoning law is valid if (i) it does not unduly restrict adult access to the material; and (ii) minors have no First Amendment right to read or view the banned material. As applied to the Internet as it exists in 1997, the "display" provision and some applications of the "indecency transmission" and "specific person" provisions fail to adhere to the first of these limiting principles by restricting adults' access to protected materials in certain circumstances. Unlike the Court, however, I would invalidate the provisions only in those circumstances.

CREATING AN ADULT ZONE

Our cases make clear that a "zoning" law is valid only if adults are still able to obtain the regulated speech. If they cannot, the law does more than simply keep children away from speech they have no right to obtain. It interferes with the rights of adults to obtain constitutionally protected speech and effectively "reduce(s) the adult population . . . to reading only what is fit for children." The First Amendment does not tolerate such interference. If the law does not unduly restrict adults' access to constitutionally protected speech, however, it may be valid. In *Ginsberg v. New York*, for example, the Court sustained a New York law that barred store owners from selling pornographic magazines to minors in part because adults could still buy those magazines.

The Court in *Ginsberg* concluded that the New York law created a constitutionally adequate adult zone simply because, on its face, it denied access only to minors. The Court did not question and therefore necessarily assumed that an adult zone, once created, would succeed in preserving adults' access while denying minors' access to the regulated speech. Before today, there was no reason to question this assumption, for the Court has previously only considered laws that operated in the physical world, a world with two characteristics that make it possible to create "adult zones": geography and identity. A minor can see an adult dance show only if he enters an establishment that provides such entertainment. And should he attempt to do so, the minor will not be able to conceal completely his identity (or, consequently, his age). Thus, the twin characteristics of geography and identity enable the establishment's proprietor to prevent children from entering the establishment, but to let adults inside.

Steve Kelley/Copley News Service. Reprinted with permission.

The electronic world is fundamentally different. Because it is no more than the interconnection of electronic pathways, cyberspace allows speakers and listeners to mask their identities. Cyberspace undeniably reflects some form of geography; chat rooms and Web sites, for example, exist at fixed "locations" on the Internet. Since users can transmit and receive messages on the Internet without revealing anything about their identities or ages, however, it is not currently possible to exclude persons from accessing certain messages on the basis of their identity.

GATEWAY TECHNOLOGY DOES NOT YET EXIST
Cyberspace differs from the physical world in another basic way: cyberspace is malleable. Thus, it is possible to construct

barriers in cyberspace and use them to screen for identity, making cyberspace more like the physical world and, consequently, more amenable to zoning laws. This transformation of cyberspace is already under way. Internet speakers (users who post material on the Internet) have begun to zone cyberspace itself through the use of "gateway" technology. Such technology requires Internet users to enter information about themselves, perhaps an adult identification number or a credit card number, before they can access certain areas of cyberspace, much like a bouncer checks a person's driver's license before admitting him to a nightclub. . . .

Despite this progress, the transformation of cyberspace is not complete. Although gateway technology has been available on the World Wide Web for some time now, it is not available to all Web speakers, and is just now becoming technologically feasible for chat rooms and USENET newsgroups. Gateway technology is not ubiquitous in cyberspace, and because without it "there is no means of age verification," cyberspace still remains largely unzoned and unzoneable. . . .

Although the prospects for the eventual zoning of the Internet appear promising, I agree with the Court that we must evaluate the constitutionality of the C.D.A. as it applies to the Internet as it exists today. Given the present state of cyberspace, I agree with the Court that the "display" provision cannot pass muster. Until gateway technology is available throughout cyberspace, and it is not in 1997, a speaker cannot be reasonably assured that the speech he displays will reach only adults because it is impossible to confine speech to an "adult zone." Thus, the only way for a speaker to avoid liability under the C.D.A. is to refrain completely from using indecent speech. But this forced silence impinges on the First Amendment right of adults to make and obtain this speech and, for all intents and purposes "reduce(s) the adult population (on the Internet) to reading only what is fit for children." As a result, the "display" provision cannot withstand scrutiny.

Parts of the C.D.A. Are Not Unconstitutional

The "indecency transmission" and "specific person" provisions present a closer issue, for they are not unconstitutional in all of their applications. As discussed above, the "indecency transmission" provision makes it a crime to transmit knowingly an indecent message to a person the sender knows is under 18 years of age. The "specific person" provision proscribes the same conduct, although it does not as explicitly require the sender to know that the intended recipient of his indecent message is a minor. Appellant urges the Court to construe the provision to impose such a knowledge requirement, and I would do so.

So construed, both provisions are constitutional as applied to a conversation involving only an adult and one or more minors—e.g., when an adult speaker sends an e-mail knowing the addressee is a minor, or when an adult and minor converse by themselves or with other minors in a chat room. In this context, these provisions are no different from the law we sustained in Ginsberg. Restricting what the adult may say to the minors in no way restricts the adult's ability to communicate with other adults. He is not prevented from speaking indecently to other adults in a chat room . . . and he remains free to send indecent e-mails to other adults. The relevant universe contains only one adult, and the adult in that universe has the power to refrain from using indecent speech and consequently to keep all such speech within the room in an "adult" zone.

The analogy to Ginsberg breaks down, however, when more than one adult is a party to the conversation. If a minor enters a chat room otherwise occupied by adults, the C.D.A. effectively requires the adults in the room to stop using indecent speech. If they did not, they could be prosecuted under the "indecency transmission" and "specific person" provisions for any indecent statements they make to the group, since they would be transmitting an indecent message to specific persons, one of whom is a minor. The C.D.A. is therefore akin to a law that makes it a crime for a bookstore owner to sell pornographic magazines to anyone once a minor enters his store. Even assuming such a law might be constitutional in the physical world as a reasonable alternative to excluding minors completely from the store, the absence of any means of excluding minors from chat rooms in cyberspace restricts the rights of adults to engage in indecent speech in those rooms. The "indecency transmission" and "specific person" provisions share this defect.

But these two provisions do not infringe on adults' speech in all situations. And . . . I do not find that the provisions are overbroad in the sense that they restrict minors' access to a substantial amount of speech that minors have the right to read and view. Accordingly, the C.D.A. can be applied constitutionally in some situations.

> "Unless . . . adequate protection for copyrighted works is insured, the vast communications network will not reach its full potential as a true, global marketplace."

INTELLECTUAL PROPERTY RIGHTS MUST BE PROTECTED

Working Group on Intellectual Property Rights

The Working Group on Intellectual Property Rights was established by President Clinton in 1993 to examine U.S. copyright laws as they applied to the National Information Infrastructure (NII) and to recommend any necessary changes. In the following viewpoint, the group contends that copyright laws must be strengthened because computer networks make it easy, cheap, and quick to copy and distribute information illicitly. If intellectual property rights are not updated and protected, the group maintains, then many content providers will find it economically unfeasible to publish information on the Internet.

As you read, consider the following questions:

1. In the Working Group's view, what must an effective intellectual property law do?
2. According to the authors, what will happen to creativity if intellectual property is not protected?
3. What are some of the ways that businesses are already charging for information on the Internet, according to the authors?

Reprinted from "Intellectual Property and the National Information Infrastructure: The Report of the Working Group on Intellectual Property Rights," as it appeared in the December 1996 *Congressional Digest* under the title "Copyright Protection and Technology: The National Information Infrastructure."

A dvances in technology particularly affect the operation and effectiveness of copyright law. Changes in technology generate new industries and new methods for reproduction and dissemination of works and authorship, which may present new opportunities for authors but also create additional challenges.

Use of computer technology—such as digitization—and communications technology—such as fiber optic cable—have had an enormous impact on the creation, reproduction, and dissemination of copyrighted works. The merger of computer and communications technology into an integrated information technology has made possible the development of the National Information Infrastructure (NII), which will generate both unprecedented challenges and important opportunities for the copyright marketplace.

BENEFITS OF NEW TECHNOLOGIES

An information infrastructure already exists, but it is not integrated into a whole. Telephones, televisions, radios, computers, and fax machines are used every day to receive, store, process, perform, display, and transmit data, text, voice, sound, and images in homes and businesses throughout the country. Fiber optics, wires, cables, switches, routers, microwave networks, satellites, and other communications technologies currently connect telephones, computers, and fax machines. The NII of tomorrow, however, will be much more than these separate communications networks; it will integrate them into an advanced high-speed, interactive, broadband, digital communications system.

The NII can increase access to a greater amount and variety of information and entertainment resources that can be delivered quickly and economically from and to virtually anywhere in the world in the blink of an eye. For instance, hundreds of channels of "television" programming, thousands of musical recordings, and literally millions of "magazines" and "books" can be made available to homes and businesses across the United States and around the world.

Individuals and entities that heretofore have been predominantly consumers of works can now become authors and providers through the NII. It can put easier, more sophisticated communication and publishing tools in the hands of the public, increasing the ability to communicate with, and disseminate works of authorship to, others.

An effective intellectual property regime must (1) ensure that users have access to the broadest feasible variety of works by (2) recognizing the legitimate rights and commercial expectations of persons and entities whose works are used in the NII environment.

We are faced with significant changes in technology that upset the balance that currently exists under the Copyright Act of 1976.

Some assert that copyright protection should be reduced in the NII environment. The public wants information to be free and unencumbered on the NII, it is argued, and the law should reflect the public interest. Without doubt, this is a valid concern.

Information *per se* should not be protected by copyright law, nor is it. Facts and ideas from any work of authorship may be freely copied and distributed; the Copyright Act expressly excludes such information from the scope of the protection it accords. The copyright law should also serve the public interest, and it does. While at first blush, it may appear to be in the public interest to reduce the protection granted works and to allow unfettered use by the public, such an analysis is incomplete. Protection of works of authorship provides the stimulus for creativity, thus leading to the availability of works of literature, culture, art, and entertainment that the public desires and that form the backbone of our economy and political discourse. If these works are not protected, then the marketplace will not support their creation and dissemination, and the public will not receive the benefit of their existence or be able to have unrestricted use of the ideas and information they convey.

Others assert that technological advances justify reduced protection. Since computer networks now make unauthorized reproduction, adaptation, distribution, and other uses of protected works so incredibly easy, it is argued, the law should legitimize those uses or face widespread flouting. This argument is not valid. Technology makes many things possible. Computer networks can be and have been used to embezzle large sums of money and commit other crimes. Yet these acts are prohibited by law.

DOES CYBERSPACE NEED DIFFERENT LAWS?

Finally, there are those who argue that intellectual property laws of any country are inapplicable to works on the NII because all activity using these infrastructures takes place in "cyberspace," a sovereignty unto itself that should be self-governed by its inhabitants, individuals who, it is suggested, will rely on their own ethics to determine what uses of works, if any, are improper.

First, this argument relies on the fantasy that users of the Internet, for instance, are somehow transported to "chat rooms" and other locations, such as virtual libraries. While such conceptualization helps to put in material terms what is considered rather abstract, activity on the Internet takes place neither in outer space nor in parallel, virtual locations. Satellite, broadcast, fax, and telephone transmissions have not been thought to be outside the jurisdiction of the nations from which or to which they are sent. Computer network transmissions have no distinguishing characteristics warranting such other-world treatment.

FEW RULES IN CYBERSPACE

At the moment, there are few rules in cyberspace. The legal status of electronic copyright is still vague, as are the legal and practical issues surrounding on-line exchange and "electronic cash." There is also limited authority to enforce rules on the Internet and little capacity to punish those who violate the norms of on-line conduct. Although these problems have been well documented, they persist nevertheless. And until they are solved, cyberspace will remain a frontier town—a land of opportunities, to be sure, but also one of tremendous risks.

Debora Spar and Jeffrey J. Bussgang, *Harvard Business Review*, May/June 1996.

Nonetheless, content providers are currently experimenting with a number of business models in the networked environment, and it is already clear that a wide variety of models may coexist. Some content providers will choose not to enforce all, or any, of their rights; others may change their business practices. For instance, some newspaper publishers are selling individual articles using electronic payment mechanisms, in addition to selling subscriptions and individual issues. Some software companies are making their "client" software freely available for individual use in an effort to increase the market share of their "server" software. Some hypermedia magazine publishers on the World Wide Web are choosing to give away their product but charge sponsors for advertising space. A number of information service providers are charging for the use of the search engines that add value to freely available public domain content.

Some content providers will not be motivated by any commercial considerations. For instance, certain scientific communities are working together to create archives of freely available electronic pre-prints on the Internet. The copyright law allows copyright owners to exercise the rights granted to them, to license their rights to others, or to give them away. Those creators who wish to dedicate their works to the public domain may, of course, do so notwithstanding the availability of protection under the Copyright Act. Nothing in the law prevents those who do not wish to claim copyright from waiving their rights and allowing unrestricted reproduction, distribution, and other use of their words. Indeed, notices to that effect are not uncommon on the Internet.

COPYRIGHT PROTECTION IS NECESSARY

The absence on the NII of copyrighted works for which authors do not wish to exercise their rights—fully or to some limited extent—under the copyright law, of course, would not necessarily result in its demise. The Internet, for instance, could continue to serve as a communications tool and resource for government, public domain, and works of willing authors. However, unless the framework for legitimate commerce is preserved and adequate protection for copyrighted works is ensured, the vast communications network will not reach its full potential as a true, global marketplace.

Copyright protection is not an obstacle in the way of the success of the NII; it is an essential component. Effective copyright protection is a fundamental way to promote the availability of works to the public.

Preserving the framework does not require, however, a dramatic increase in authors' rights, such as more limited or no further applicability of the fair use doctrine in the NII environment. The Working Group believes that weakening copyright owners' rights in the NII is not in the public interest; nor would a dramatic increase in their rights be justified. With no more than minor clarification and limited amendment, the Copyright Act will provide the necessary balance of protection of rights—and limitations on those rights—to promote the progress of science and the useful arts.

> "Information providers already have
> lots of ways to protect their
> investments—existing copyright
> law, controlled access, encryption."

INTELLECTUAL PROPERTY RIGHTS DO NOT NEED NEW PROTECTIONS

James Boyle

In the following viewpoint, James Boyle argues that proposed new copyright laws meant to protect intellectual property on the Internet will unfairly limit the legitimate use of information by Internet browsers. Overly restrictive intellectual property laws will prevent people from distributing information, he contends, and will stifle future intellectual innovations. Boyle is a law professor at American University in Washington, D.C., and the author of *Shamans, Software and Spleens*.

As you read, consider the following questions:

1. In Boyle's opinion, what is the promise of the Internet?
2. According to the author, what is the "fair use" standard set by the Supreme Court?
3. What is the implicit quid pro quo of intellectual property rights, in the author's opinion?

What if the ground rules for the information society were written and no one noticed? What if they were bad? Given the current frenzy about the Internet, technology stocks and cyberporn, this scenario is hard to believe. But the ground rules have been written, almost no one noticed and they are bad—really bad.

In September 1995 the Clinton administration released a white paper on intellectual property on the Internet. Sens. Orrin Hatch, a Utah Republican, and Patrick Leahy, a Vermont Democrat, have introduced its recommendations as S 1284. The white paper says it is just a "minor clarification" of the law.

COPYRIGHT PROTECTION AND THE INTERNET

In fact, under its bland surface, the white paper is an astoundingly radical measure. It makes *reading* an Internet document a copyright violation, cuts off from the information highway those who cannot afford to license information and dramatically restricts the fair use of copyrighted material. In an Orwellian twist, it will become a copyright violation—and sometimes a federal crime—to circumvent the electronic mechanisms that monitor your use of information products, even to protect your own privacy. On-line providers will strictly be liable for violations of copyright by their members. The promise of the information superhighway—universal access, free exchange of information, the promotion of technological innovation, free speech and personal privacy—would be replaced by the opposite. And this is being done in the name of saving the Internet, which is growing exponentially, largely because it isn't stunted by protectionist rules such as those urged by Hatch and Leahy.

How did this happen? It started with a fantasy about the state of the current law.

The white paper is supposed to give us an objective depiction of the law so we can judge whether changes are necessary. Unfortunately, it doesn't. The summary of the current state of intellectual-property law actually is a brief for publishing interests. It makes a point of concentrating on any court case or statutory provision that extends the reach of intellectual-property rights while minimizing or (more troublingly still) omitting altogether the countervailing decisions, policies and doctrines. This would be similar to a summary of attitudes toward birth control that quoted only those of the Roman Catholic Church.

Take the white paper's surprising assertion that, under current law, one copies a document simply by reading it on a computer screen. The argument is that the computer has to load the document into its random-access memory before displaying it. This copy disappears the moment one goes to the next screen or turns off the computer, but the white paper contends that no use is too small to pay for. Thus, browsing becomes a copyright violation and the information superhighway turns into an information toll road. Tell those third-graders to have their credit cards ready.

Some courts have taken this position, but it has been widely criticized. Would Congress really want to give copyright-holders exclusive control of reading and viewing? In fact, Congress' own legislative report on the current copyright statute gave as an example of a noninfringing reproduction the temporary display of images on a screen. The white paper fails to mention these inconvenient facts.

To give another example, the right to make fair use of copyrighted material is so important to free speech and future creative activity that the Supreme Court established an implicit presumption that noncommercial private copying is fair use. Subsequent cases have modified this standard but the thrust of it remains. According to the white paper, however, any time one uses copyrighted material that could have been licensed from its owner, there is the presumption of a copyright violation. It's hard to imagine a more dramatic shift—from presumed innocent to presumed guilty. Is this a minor clarification? Here too, the author of the white paper seems to think so.

An Unbalanced Law

The picture of the law the white paper presents is so unbalanced that if it were to be given in a lawyer's brief it would come close to infringing upon the ethical rule that a lawyer must reveal contrary cases and statutes. When my students ask me what this means, I give them two no-brainer examples. If you argue that a statute says one thing, but the legislative report says the opposite, it's probably an ethical violation to conceal the contradiction. If there is a body of law that contradicts your argument and you don't mention it, you are heading for disbarment. Those are the rules for advocates, who have an ethical duty to make the strongest case possible for their clients. The white paper is supposed to be an objective statement of the law; it should do better. A *generous* interpretation of this performance is that it is careless.

The sponsors of the legislation are not responsible for these flaws, of course. They are introducing only the white paper's legislative proposals, saying they see them as the beginning of a debate about the needs of the 'Net. But the proposals embody the white paper's philosophical biases and its inaccurate account of what the law is now. That could twist the resulting debate. Worse still, courts might presume that Congress agreed with the white paper and its one-sided fantasy would become the law without ever having been exposed to the skepticism it so richly deserves.

©1994 Harley Schwadron. Reprinted with permission.

Who will this bill help? Not writers and creators. The bill would accelerate the recent tendency to shift the balance against authors and in favor of publishers. Would the bill be good for on-line service providers—ranging from America Online to the altruistic private bulletin-board operator? Hardly. It makes them strictly liable for copyright violations they can't control. Would this encourage a flourishing world of on-line services? No. It will drive the private individuals out and force the companies to monitor their clients: A kind of privatized Big Brother. Would the bill be good for the computer industry? No. It tries to pick the winners in the information economy. Is it good for education or for libraries—areas the Clinton administration identified as a priority for the information superhighway? No. In fact, it would impede public access and distance learning. How could it be good for civil liberties, when it encourages extensive private and public surveillance of cyberspace? How could it be good for consumers—whose fair-use rights are being nationalized and turned over to the large-content providers? It takes an astounding bill to harm so many constituencies. How did we get this one?

There are many answers to the question. For some it is that the chief author of the report, Bruce Lehman, the commissioner of patents and trademarks, used to be employed as a lawyer by the software industry and is seizing this opportunity to write that industry's wish list into law under the guise of a minor clarification. For others it is that Hollywood and the record industry contributed lots of money to the Democrats. (The giant movie and record industries are pondering uneasily how to deal with the information superhighway. The white paper rewrites the rules of the road to give them a break. By doing so, it forecloses a lot of the 'Net's innovative potential for the sake of a corporate-welfare program. It's like dealing with the introduction of movable type by insisting each letter be hand-inked by a professional scribe.) The influence of money and power always is a good explanation for legislation that otherwise doesn't make sense, but there are more creditable reasons why some serious legislators and an administration nominally committed to universal access would buy this kind of nonsense.

INTELLECTUAL PROPERTY IS UNFAMILIAR TO MOST

First, intellectual property is unfamiliar territory for most people. It's easy for a smart lawyer to make arguments about property rights that sound reasonable but don't really make sense. Intellectual-property rights are limited monopolies conferred in order to produce present and future public benefits. For the purposes of producing those benefits, the limitations on the right—such as the fact that all of us are allowed to make fair use of copyrighted material for news reporting or educational purposes, or that programmers can decompile another company's computer program so as to produce better innovations themselves—are just as important as the grant of the right itself. It's the implicit quid pro quo of intellectual property: We will give you this valuable legal monopoly, backed by state power; in return, we will design the contours of your right so as to encourage a variety of socially valuable uses.

The white paper's strategy is to talk as though the rights of copyright holders were absolute and thus to squeeze the limitations on those rights out of existence. Lehman wants to give copyright-holders the quid while claiming that the quo is a tax or forced subsidy. Only the unfamiliarity of intellectual property conceals the ludicrousness of the argument. It's as if a developer had negotiated a fat package of cash grants and tax breaks as the price of building a stadium in Washington, but then wanted to claim the benefits of the deal while insisting that to make him fulfill his side of the bargain would be to confer a subsidy on the city.

Second, the digital environment is unfamiliar and legislators are rushing to regulate it, assuming that they know exactly what effects the technology will have. A little history is instructive. Fifteen years ago the TV and movie companies were screaming that a new technology—the videocassette recorder—would destroy their business. They wanted a tax put on each VCR to compensate them. Luckily for them, Congress and the Supreme Court disagreed. Thanks in part to the availability of cheap, untaxed VCRs, the video business exploded. Video rentals saved Hollywood.

COPYRIGHTS AND INNOVATION

The Internet makes copying easier, but it also makes distribution and access cheaper so that a smaller initial investment can produce larger returns. Should the level of property protection be raised or lowered? Should it be raised in some places and lowered in others? Congress needs to be careful. Any sophisticated information economist will tell you that a level of intellectual-property rights that is too high will stifle innovation just as effectively as a level of intellectual-property rights that is too low. Information providers already have lots of ways to protect their investments—existing copyright law, controlled access, encryption. They are inventing new ways every day. Who would have thought that Netscape could become the hottest stock on the market by giving away its software? The point is that the environment is complicated and, like most markets, more inventive than any single person. Right now, it is flourishing both economically and culturally; the last thing it needs is to be "saved" by Congress. We should leave it alone until the cyberdust settles a little.

Sens. Hatch and Leahy have distinguished records in intellectual-property legislation, but in this case they should heed the most important rule of public policy. It comes from the Hippocratic oath, and it says: "First, do no harm."

PERIODICAL BIBLIOGRAPHY

The following articles have been selected to supplement the diverse views presented in this chapter. Addresses are provided for periodicals not indexed in the *Readers' Guide to Periodical Literature*, the *Alternative Press Index*, the *Social Sciences Index*, or the *Index to Legal Periodicals and Books*.

David Banisar	"Big Brother Goes High-Tech," *Covert Action Quarterly*, Spring 1996.
Colin Beavan	"They're Watching You," *Esquire*, August 1997.
David Brin	"Privacy Is History—Get over It, an interview with David Brin," interview by Sheldon Teitelbaum, *Wired*, February 1996. Available from 520 Third St., 4th Fl., San Francisco, CA 94107.
Lynn Darling	"Dear Ravager, I've Never Done This Before," *Esquire*, July 1997.
Lawrence K. Grossman	"Reshaping Political Values in the Information Age," *Vital Speeches of the Day*, January 15, 1997.
Steven Levy	"On the Net, Anything Goes," *Newsweek*, July 7, 1997.
Edward J. Markey	"A Privacy Safety Net," *Technology Review*, August/September 1997.
Peter F. McCloskey	"Meeting the Demand for Global Information," *USA Today*, January 1996.
Ralph Nader	"Digital Democracy in Action," *Forbes ASAP*, December 2, 1996.
Adam Newey	"Networking for God," *Index on Censorship*, July/August 1996.
Norman Ornstein and Amy Schenkenberg	"The Promise and Perils of Cyberdemocracy," *American Enterprise*, March/April 1996.
Joshua Quittner	"Invasion of Privacy," *Time*, August 25, 1997.
Joshua Quittner	"Unshackling Net Speech," *Time*, July 7, 1997.
Glen Roberts	"Text, Spies, and Cyberspace, and Interview with Glen Roberts," interview by Vicki Quade, *Human Rights*, Spring 1996. Available from
Pamela Samuelson	"The Copyright Grab," *Wired*, January 1996.

Andrew L. Shapiro   "Privacy for Sale: Peddling Data on the Internet," *Nation*, June 23, 1997.

David Wagner   "High-Tech Snoops Get Real Personal," *Insight*, August 19, 1996. Available from 3600 New York Ave. NE, Washington, DC 20002.

Thomas E. Weber   "Browsers Beware: The Web Is Watching," *Wall Street Journal*, June 27, 1996.

George F. Will   "Sex, Fat, and Responsibility," *Newsweek*, July 7, 1997.

FOR FURTHER DISCUSSION

CHAPTER 1

1. Michael Spindler identifies himself as the former president and chief operating officer of Apple Computer Corporation. Does this fact influence your assessment of his argument that information technology can benefit society? Explain your answer.

2. David Shenk contends that the boom in computer and communications technology has inundated society with excess data, creating information overload. Paul Levinson maintains that society is actually suffering from information underload—that is, a scarcity of technology that can help humans process new information. What evidence does each author present to support his argument? Which author's evidence do you find more convincing? Why?

CHAPTER 2

1. The National Academy of Sciences argues that schools should use technological innovations to enhance learning and to prepare students for the workplaces of the future. Gertrude Himmelfarb contends that some information technology—such as computer networks—may actually hinder the careful, slow thought required for intellectual inquiry. In each viewpoint, try to find two supporting arguments with which you personally agree. Why do you agree with them?

2. Chris Morton states that schools should emphasize computer-based education. How does Todd Oppenheimer respond to this contention? Whose argument is more convincing? Why?

3. William A. Wulf and Majid Tehranian offer differing opinions on the importance of the university as a physical setting. On what points do these two authors agree? On what points do they disagree?

CHAPTER 3

1. This chapter lists several possible ways in which information technology could transform the world of work. Consider each alternative and then list arguments for and against the validity of each one. Note whether the arguments are based on facts, values, emotions, or other considerations. If you believe any alternative is not viable, explain why.

2. Kim Nauer maintains that the telecommunications industry should be required to provide universal access to its services to ensure that low-income and minority neighborhoods receive

information-age technologies. Steve Gibson contends that such universal-service requirements would be restrictive and unnecessary. Which viewpoint do you agree with, and why?

CHAPTER 4

1. Reed Karaim argues that new technologies have brought about a loss of individual privacy. Jeffrey Obser contends that the desire for personal privacy has necessitated the detailed record keeping made possible by technological innovations. How do the arguments of these two authors reflect differing views on the nature of privacy? Explain your answer, using examples from the viewpoints.

2. John Paul Stevens argues that banning indecent material and pornography from the Internet in order to protect children is unconstitutional. Sandra Day O'Connor contends that blocking minors' access to indecent material on computer networks could be considered constitutional. Compare the opinions presented in these two viewpoints, then formulate your own argument concerning free speech and children's access to obscene material on the Internet.

3. The Working Group on Intellectual Property Rights contends that copyright laws must be strengthened to protect intellectual property on the Internet. James Boyle maintains that new copyright restrictions would unfairly limit the use and distribution of information by Internet browsers. Does Boyle's viewpoint effectively refute the arguments put forth by the Working Group on Intellectual Property Rights? Why or why not?

ORGANIZATIONS TO CONTACT

The editors have compiled the following list of organizations concerned with the issues debated in this book. The descriptions are derived from materials provided by the organizations. All have publications or information available for interested readers. The list was compiled on the date of publication of the present volume; the information provided may change. Be aware that many organizations take several weeks or longer to respond to inquiries, so allow as much time as possible.

Center for Civic Networking (CCN)

PO Box 53152, Washington, DC 20009
(202) 362-3831 • fax: (202) 244-4380
e-mail: ccn@civicnet.org • web address: http://www.civicnet.org

CCN is dedicated to promoting the use of information technology and infrastructure to improve access to information and the delivery of government services, broaden citizen participation in government, and stimulate economic and community development. It conducts policy research and analysis and consults with government and nonprofit organizations. The center publishes various papers and articles on-line, such as The Internet and the Poor and Building Community Information Infrastructure.

Center for Democracy and Technology (CDT)

1001 G St. NW, Suite 700E, Washington, DC 20001
(202) 637-9800 • fax: (202) 637-0968
e-mail: info@cdt.org • web address: http://www.cdt.org

CDT's mission is to develop public policy solutions that advance constitutional civil liberties and democratic values in new computer and communications media. Pursuing its mission through policy research, public education, and coalition building, the center works to increase citizens' privacy and the public's control over the use of personal information held by government and other institutions. Its publications include issue briefs; policy papers; and CDT Policy Posts, an on-line occasional publication that covers issues regarding the civil liberties of those using the information highway.

Center for Media Education (CME)

1511 K St. NW, Suite 518, Washington, DC 20005
(202) 628-2620 • fax: (202) 628-2554
e-mail: cme@cme.org • web address: http://www.cme.org/cme

CME is a public interest group concerned with media and telecommunications issues, including educational television for children, universal access to the information highway, and the development and ownership of information services. Its projects include the Campaign for Kids TV, which seeks to improve children's education; the Future of Media, concerning the information highway; and the Telecommunications Policy Roundtable of monthly meetings of non-profit organizations. CME publishes reports on-line, such as *Web of Deception: Threats to Children from Online Marketing*, and the quarterly newsletter *InfoActive Kids*.

Computing Research Association (CRA)
1100 17th St. NW, Suite 507, Washington, DC 20036-4632
(202) 234-2111 • fax: (202) 667-1056
e-mail: info@cra.org • web address: http://www.cra.org

CRA seeks to strengthen research and education in the computing fields, expand opportunities for women and minorities, and educate the public and policy makers on the importance of computing research. CRA's publications include the bimonthly newsletter *Computing Research News*.

Electronic Frontier Foundation (EFF)
1550 Bryant St., Suite 725, San Francisco, CA 94103-4832
(415) 436-9333 • fax: (415) 436-9993
e-mail: ask@eff.org • web address: http://www.eff.org

EFF aims to promote a better understanding of telecommunications issues. It fosters awareness of civil liberties issues arising from advancements in computer-based communications media and supports litigation to preserve, protect, and extend First Amendment rights in computing and telecommunications technologies. EFF's publications include the quarterly newsletter *EFFector Online* and on-line bulletins and publications, including *Stop the Government from Building Big Brother into the Internet*.

Electronic Privacy Information Center (EPIC)
666 Pennsylvania Ave. SE, Suite 301, Washington, DC 20003
(202) 544-9240 • fax: (202) 547-5482
e-mail: info@epic.org • web address: http://www.epic.org

EPIC advocates a public right to electronic privacy. It sponsors educational and research programs, compiles statistics, and conducts litigation. Its publications include the biweekly electronic newsletter *EPIC Alert* and various on-line reports.

Interactive Services Association (ISA)
8403 Colesville Rd., Suite 865, Silver Springs, MD 20910
(301) 495-4955 • fax: (301) 495-4959
e-mail: isa@isa.net • web address: http://www.isa.net

ISA is a trade association representing more than three hundred companies in advertising, broadcasting, and other areas involving the delivery of telecommunications-based services. It has six councils, including Interactive Marketing and Interactive Television, covering the interactive media industry. The association publishes various on-line press releases and the weekly newsletter *Publications* (delivered by fax or e-mail), which summarizes current news stories and public policy developments.

International Computer Security Association (ICSA)
1200 Walnut Bottom Rd., Carlisle, PA 17013
(717) 258-1816 • (800) 488-4595 • fax: (717) 243-8642
web address: http://www.icsa.net

ICSA offers information and opinions on computer security issues. It strives to improve computer security by disseminating information and certifying security products. The association publishes the bi-monthly *ICSA Newsletter*.

International Society for Technology in Education (ISTE)
1787 Agate St., Eugene, OR 97403
(800) 336-5191 • fax: (541) 346-5890
e-mail: cust_svc@ccmail.uoregon.edu
web address: http://www.iste.org

ISTE is a multinational organization composed of teachers, administrators, and computer and curriculum coordinators. It facilitates the exchange of information and resources between international policy makers and professional organizations related to the fields of education and technology. The society also encourages research on and evaluation of the use of technology in education. It publishes the journal *Learning and Leading with Technology* eight times a year, the newsletter *ISTE Update* seven times a year, and the quarterly *Journal of Research on Computing in Education*.

Internet Society
12020 Sunrise Valley Dr., Suite 210, Reston, VA 20191
(703) 648-9888 • fax: (703) 648-9887
e-mail: isoc@isoc.org • web address: http://www.isoc.org

A group of technologists, developers, educators, researchers, government representatives, and businesspeople, the Internet Society supports the development and dissemination of standards for the Internet and works to ensure global cooperation and coordination for the Internet and related technologies and applications. It publishes the bimonthly magazine *On the Internet*.

SafeSurf

16032 Sherman Wy., Suite 58, Van Nuys, CA 91406
(818) 902-9390 • fax: (818) 902-1928
e-mail: safesurf@safesurf.com • web address: http://www.safesurf.com

The goal of SafeSurf is to prevent children from accessing adult material—including pornography—on the Internet. It maintains that standards must be implemented on the Internet to protect children. SafeSurf reviews entertainment products such as children's computer games and awards a seal of excellence to exceptional products. The organization publishes the quarterly newsletter *SafeSurf News*.

Special Interest Group for Computers and Society (SIGCAS)

c/o Association for Computing Machinery
1515 Broadway, 17th Fl., New York, NY 10036
(212) 869-7440 • fax: (212) 944-1318

SIGCAS is composed of computer and physical scientists, professionals, and other individuals interested in issues concerning the effects of computers on society. It aims to inform the public of issues concerning computers and society through such publications as the quarterly newsletter *Computers and Society*.

United Federation of ChildSafe Web Sites (UFCWS)

1555 W. Fifth St., Suite 265, Oxnard, CA 93030
(805) 984-2538
e-mail: madmonk@childsafe.com
web address: http://www.childsafe.com

The federation advocates responsible free speech and strives to make the World Wide Web a more suitable medium for children. UFCWS developed the Internet ChildSafe Certification Standard to guarantee parents that their children are accessing positive and productive Web content. The federation publishes the monthly electronic publication *Positive Image* and updates an electronic newsletter daily, both of which can be accessed on their web site.

Voters Telecommunications Watch (VTW)

233 Court St., #2, Brooklyn, NY 11201-6540
(718) 596-2851
e-mail: vtw@vtw.org • web address: http://www.vtw.org

VTW is a coalition of civil liberties organizations that actively participates in the democratic and legislative processes to promote civil liberties for telecommunications users. It recommends legislation, monitors the positions and voting records of elected officials, and informs the public about relevant issues. VTW publishes *VTW-Announce*, a weekly on-line newsletter that chronicles federal legislation affecting telecommunications and civil liberties. Subscribe by sending e-mail to vtw-announce-request@vtw.org.

BIBLIOGRAPHY OF BOOKS

John Brockman	*Digerati: Encounters with the Cyber Elite.* Emeryville, CA: Publishers Group, 1996.
Tal Brooke, ed.	*Virtual Gods.* Eugene, OR: Harvest House, 1997.
Martin Campbell-Kelly and William Aspray	*Computer: A History of the Information Machine.* New York: BasicBooks, 1996.
Jim Cummins and Dennis Sayers	*Brave New Schools: Challenging Cultural Illiteracy Through Global Learning Networks.* New York: St. Martin's, 1995.
Peter J. Denning and Robert M. Metcalfe	*Beyond Calculation: The Next Fifty Years of Computing.* New York: Copernicus Books, 1997.
Michael L. Dertouzos	*What Will Be: How the New World of Information Will Change Our Lives.* San Francisco: HarperSanFrancisco, 1997.
David G. Garson and G. David Garson	*Computer Technology and Social Issues.* Wilmington, DE: Idea Group, 1995.
Bill Gates	*The Road Ahead.* New York: Viking, 1995.
Paul Gilster	*Digital Literacy.* New York: Wiley, 1997.
Steven Johnson	*Interface Culture: How New Technology Transforms the Way We Create and Communicate.* San Francisco: HarperSanFrancisco, 1997.
Rob Kling, ed.	*Computerization and Controversy: Value Conflicts and Social Choices.* San Diego, CA: Academic Press, 1996.
Pierre Levy and Robert Bononno	*Collective Intelligence: Mankind's Emerging World in Cyberspace.* New York: Plenum Press, 1997.
John Naisbitt	*Megatrends 2000.* New York: Avon, 1996.
Nicholas Negroponte	*Being Digital.* New York: Knopf, 1995.
O'Reilly & Associates, eds.	*Internet and Society.* Cambridge, MA: Harvard University Press, 1997.
Charles Platt	*Anarchy Online.* New York: HarperCollins, 1997.
David Porter, ed.	*Internet Culture.* New York: Routledge, 1997.
Gregory J.E. Rawlins	*Slaves of the Machine: The Quickening of Computer Technology.* Cambridge, MA: MIT Press, 1997.
Gene I. Rochlin	*Trapped in the Net: The Unanticipated Consequences of Computerization.* Princeton, NJ: Princeton University Press, 1997.
Richard S. Rosenberg	*The Social Impact of Computers.* San Diego, CA: Academic Press, 1997.

Theodore Roszak

The Cult of Information: A New-Luddite Treatise on High Tech, Artificial Intelligence, and the True Art of Thinking. Berkeley and Los Angeles: University of California Press, 1994.

Herbert I. Schiller

Information Inequality: The Deepening Social Crisis in America. New York: Routledge, 1996.

David Shenk

Data Smog: Surviving the Information Glut. San Francisco: HarperSanFrancisco, 1997.

Richard A. Spinello

Case Studies in Information and Computer Ethics. Scarborough, ON: Prentice Hall, 1997.

Clifford Stoll

Silicon Snake Oil: Second Thoughts on the Information Highway. New York: Doubleday, 1995.

Don Tapscott

Growing Up Digital: The Rise of the Net Generation. New York: McGraw-Hill, 1997.

Don Tapscott and Ann Cavoukian

Who Knows: Safeguarding Your Privacy in a Networked World. New York: McGraw-Hill, 1997.

Alvin Toffler and Heidi Toffler

Creating a New Civilization: The Politics of the Third Wave. Atlanta: Turner, 1995.

Ellen Ullman

Close to the Machine: Technophilia and Its Discontents. San Francisco: City Lights Books, 1997.

Jonathan Wallace and Mark Mangan

Sex, Laws, and Cyber-Space: Freedom and Censorship on the Frontiers of the Online Revolution. New York: Henry Holt, 1996.

David B. Whittle

Cyberspace: The Human Dimension. New York: W.H. Freeman, 1997.

William Wresch

Disconnected: Haves and Have-Nots in the Information Age. New Brunswick, NJ: Rutgers University Press, 1996.

INDEX

James, William, 38
Japan, 96
Jobs, Steven, 70-71
just-in-time (JIT) systems, 98-99, 108, 125

Kahn, Tom, 115
Kant, Immanuel, 37, 38
Karaim, Reed, 151
Keyworth, Jay, 19
Kiesler, Sara, 97
Kinsley, Michael, 53-54
Klaas, Polly, 155
Kline, David, 137
Kolmar Laboratories, 98
Krause, Audrie, 137

Labor Department, U.S., 114
Leahy, Patrick, 182, 186
Legal Aid Society of Dayton, Ohio, 138
Lehman, Bruce, 185
Lehtonen, Jaako, 28
Lenzner, Terry, 154
Lesgold, Alan, 67
Levenson, William, 65
Levinson, Paul, 32
Lewis, Dell, 141
libraries, 75, 84, 135, 136, 184
  and organized information, 38
Limbaugh, Rush, 86, 87

Manhattan Institute, 143
Marien, Michael, 21
Massachusetts, 60, 66, 72
Massachusetts Institute of Technology, 67
  Laboratory for Computer Science, 29
McClintock, Robert, 133
McDonnell Douglas, 106
McKinsey & Co., 67
McLuhan, Marshall, 50
Mead, Dana G., 121
Measelle, Richard L., 47
Medved, Michael, 51
Meier, Richard, 25, 26
Meiksins, Peter, 106
Microsoft, 144
Miller, Edward, 69
Monthly Review, 106
Moore, G.E., 33
Morton, Chris, 55
Mumford, Lewis, 36

NAIRU (non-accelerating inflation rate of unemployment), 124, 125
Naked Society, The (Packard), 161
Nation, The, 138
National Academy of Sciences, 44

National Association of Manufacturers (NAM), 121, 127
National Economic Council, 141
National Geographic, 100
National Information Infrastructure (NII), 141, 176, 177, 178, 180
  Advisory Council, 67
National Institute of Standards and Technology (NIST), 106
National Labor Relations Board, 128
National Public Radio, 141
National Research Council, 76
Nation of Opportunity: A Final Report of the United States Advisory Council on the National Information Infrastructure, A, 37
Nauer, Kim, 131
Netscape, 186
Neuhaus, Richard John, 23
New Jersey, 66, 70
Newman, John Cardinal, 78-79, 80
New Perspectives Quarterly, 19
New Republic, 141
Newsweek, 144
New York, 60, 153
New York Times, 26, 69, 109, 122, 141
Nixon, Richard, 160, 164, 165
Noam, Eli, 29, 82, 84, 86
  on college community, 85
  on functions of university, 83
Nock, Steven L., 161
Novak, Philip, 26

Obser, Jeffrey, 159
O'Connor, Sandra Day, 171
Ofori, Kofi Asiedu, 135
Oppenheimer, Todd, 64
Orwell, George, 158, 163, 182

Packard, Vance, 161
Pentagon of Power (Mumford), 36
personal computers, (PCs), 18, 126, 144
Piaget, Jean, 37
Platt, Charles, 157
Postman, Neil, 71
printing, 50, 141
Printing Press as an Agent of Change, The (Eisenstein), 50
privacy, 101, 157, 160
  and government surveillance, 164
  history of, 153
  and isolation, 159-61
  laws unnecessary for, 162, 165
  and threat of technology, 151-52, 154, 158
    exaggeration of, 163
    and marketing databases, 155-56
  see also electronic monitoring
Privacy for Sale (Rothfeder), 154

200